5-Minute Devotions for Mom

5-MINUTE
DEVOTIONS FOR
MOM

150 Days of Peace, Prayer, and the Power of God

TERESA ANN CRISWELL

ROCKRIDGE
PRESS

For general information on our other products and services or to obtain technical support, please contact our Customer Care Department within the United States at (866) 744-2665, or outside the United States at (510) 253-0500.

Rockridge Press publishes its books in a variety of electronic and print formats. Some content that appears in print may not be available in electronic books, and vice versa.

Interior and Cover Designer: Angela Navarra
Art Producer: Karen Williams and Janice Ackerman
Editor: Lauren O'Neal and Mo Mozuch
Production Editor: Ruth Sakata Corley

Illustration: © Lisima/Creative Market

ISBN: Print 978-1-64739-830-9 | eBook 978-1-64739-527-8
R0

*To every unique daughter
of the Father God.
May you truly know
and experience
His incomprehensible
love for you.*

♡

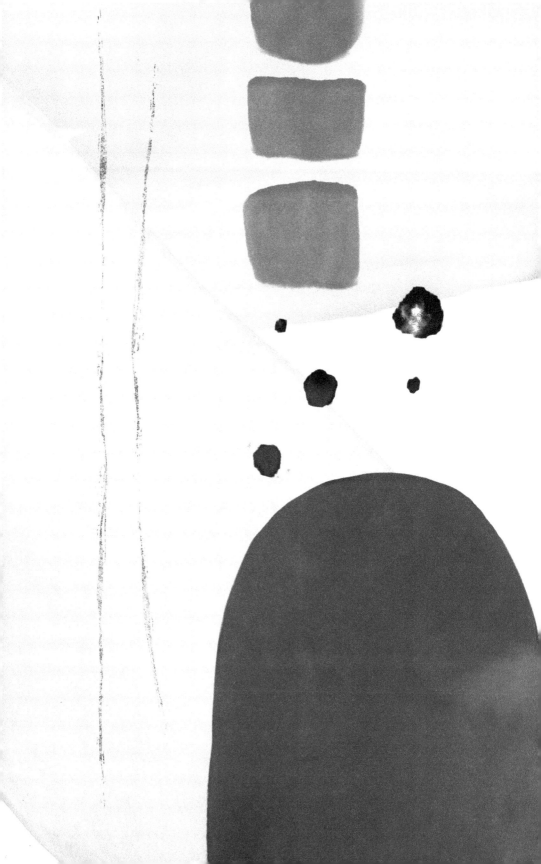

Contents

Introduction

elcome! I'm so glad you've picked up *5-Minute Devotions for Mom*, a devotional that will help you strengthen your faith and spend more time with God every day, no matter how busy you are with the daily tasks of motherhood.

These devotions are short enough to fit into your schedule, but I hope they inspire a deep dive into the heart of the Father. I pray this book stirs a love for Him in ways that overflow into how you love yourself, your family, and others. May you sense Him beckoning you to Himself. May these five minutes each day turn into a lifetime of desiring more of Him.

This book is here to simply point you upward and forward to God, so there's no right or wrong way to read it. You can read it at the same time every day (say, with coffee in the morning), or you can read it whenever you need a quick moment to pause and reconnect with God. If you have extra time or a need for guidance, you could even read several devotions in one day. My hope is that this book will help you reconnect your awareness to God at least once every day, but don't feel guilty if you miss days or "fall behind." Just know that no matter how busy or hectic your life as a mother may be, this book is waiting to point you back to the Father.

I invite you to experience God's grace that abounds and His joy that surpasses all understanding. God has you, and I'm cheering for you. Enjoy the sweet moments with the Lord that these devotionals provide, and let them draw you nearer to who He is.

Getting on Their Level

So the Word became human and made his home among us. He was full of unfailing love and faithfulness. And we have seen his glory, the glory of the Father's one and only Son.
→ John 1:14

Once, when my daughter, Tristin, was about five years old, I asked her to grab my journal for me. She was eager to help, but as she struggled to find it, I heard frustration in her small voice.

"Honey, it's right in front of you," I told her.

"Mommy, no it's not," she said, her voice rising an octave. "I don't see it."

Suddenly, I realized it was up on the kitchen counter. I walked over to her and crouched down to her level to see what she could see. Sure enough, it was in a spot she couldn't see from her height. As much as she wanted to help me, she simply couldn't from where she stood.

I've often returned to that memory as a reminder to look at someone else's situation through *their* eyes, to see what they're seeing. Jesus lived out this principle with incredible compassion. He quite literally got down "on our level" by giving up His right to be God, choosing the womb of a teenage girl over heaven. He came down to our level to call us up to those divine heights we could never imagine without our Savior. When we get down on others' levels, it's important that we endeavor to follow Jesus's example—that we see things from their perspective but encourage them toward God's higher path at the same time. In understanding others by imagining their point of view, we also begin the work of imagining others through the lens of His heart. From there, we remain in Him, being humble and getting on someone else's level, even as we encourage them toward a higher perspective—whether that means seeing from God's perspective through His Word or simply seeing over the kitchen counter.

LET'S PRAY: "Father God, I want to see through the lens of Your heart, by and through Your Holy Spirit's power. Lord, thank You for considering us even though we were yet sinners. Christ still died for us, and anyone who believes will be saved and live in You, who are Victory. In Jesus's name, amen."

Quick Yet Slow

You must all be quick to listen, slow to speak, and slow to get angry. Human anger does not produce the righteousness God desires.
→ James 1:19–20

It was one of those days when my patience was running on fumes. My son (technically my stepson, although I prefer to call him my "bonus son"), who was 13 years old at the time, did something that set me off. I was quick to run my mouth and didn't take anything into consideration, including him. I could almost instantly see his demeanor change as he crumpled with hurt and embarrassment. I remember him desperately trying to explain himself, but I wouldn't hear it. I proved all too well that my anger didn't produce anything life-giving. Instead, it seemed to demolish so much. It was one of those moments I wish I could do over again.

Looking back now, I don't even remember what my son actually did, but I feel grateful that he forgave me so quickly. It's no wonder James urges us to be quick to listen and slow to speak. Anger subsides over time. Scripture can be loud in your spirit—and yet James's words to us can still seem so quiet.

Do you notice the common theme in today's verses? Thinking of this verse and my own son, I can now clearly see that this scripture radiates from God's love for us. No matter what, God is quick yet slow. He is quick to listen as we confess our sins, and He is slow to anger as He embraces us, continuously calling us His own.

TRY THIS TODAY: Take notice of your interactions with your family, and think about them in relation to God's love and today's scripture. At the end of the day, write down the moments you quickly leaned into God for His help. Then write down the moments when you didn't. Ask God's forgiveness for the moments you didn't, and spend some time writing out how God's love could have helped you in these moments. Keep moving forward in Him.

Flourishing Results

And after you have suffered a little while,
the God of all grace, who has called you to
his eternal glory in Christ, will himself restore,
confirm, strengthen, and establish you.
→ 1 Peter 5:10

For about five years, we've had a small garden bed of roses. It started out tiny, just big enough for a few blooms. Whenever my husband has pruned them, I've been sad to see the rosebushes looking half-dead, their leaves torn away and branches cut. I even asked him whether we *have* to prune them. "Just watch," he told me. "Soon, this whole rosebush will be full of rosebuds." As much as I wanted to believe him, I still felt like he was harming them.

But today I looked outside and saw that he was right. The bush was full of beautiful blooming roses! Let the flowers in your life serve as a visual reminder from God that when life seems to strip us of our branches, it's not without purpose. God prunes and transforms us so that we may grow and bear fruit in Him.

LET'S TALK: Have you been feeling the effects of pruning in your life recently? Let go of the weariness or apprehension you may feel in response, and remember that pruning brings us closer to God's presence.

Doormat to the Red Carpet

If someone slaps you on one cheek, offer the other cheek also. → Luke 6:29

Walking through the parking lot, I saw someone familiar approaching. Suddenly, I realized it was a young woman who had, a year earlier, accused me of something I didn't do. Time seemed to slow down as we looked one another over coldly. She didn't care for me, and I sure as heck didn't care for her, either. The knot in my stomach was a clear sign that I hadn't even come close to forgiving her.

But in the following weeks, I kept thinking about that unexpected meeting, and I had an unconventional idea, inspired by today's scripture: Drop a gift off at her doorstep and leave her a kind note. The thought alone jolted my mind, and I felt a gut instinct to refuse the thought. Yet by the Father's light, my heart knew this was a "God thing" to do.

The small items I gave her weren't a lot, but I prayed hard that God's blessings would be all over that gift. I knew God was putting that scripture into action through me, urging me to exercise forgiveness in my life.

When we perform these kind acts for people we consider "enemies," we might initially feel like a doormat. From God's perspective, however, we're actually rolling out the red carpet for the King of Glory. When we allow His teachings to resonate in our way of life, He does what only He can do in and through our lives and the lives of those we're blessing.

LET'S TALK: Is there an "enemy" in your life? Do you know deep down that you must reveal the love of God to them by forgiving them? Begin praying, "Father, forgive them for they know not what they do." As you pray with earnest concern for those you struggle with, ask God what He intends for them—and then pray they discover His intentions and dreams for them.

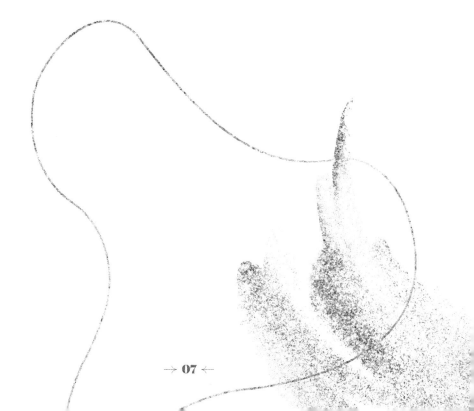

Waiting in Adoration

Never let loyalty and kindness leave you!
Tie them around your neck as a reminder.
Write them deep within your heart.
→ Proverbs 3:3

Our dog—a smooth fox terrier named Jack—lay patiently at the front door, waiting for my husband to get home from work as I walked around the house tidying up. I called out Jack's name, and he came running over, sat down when I commanded, and then went back to lie down by the front door. A few minutes later, I heard the garage opening and Jack whining excitedly. Next, I heard the key turning in the lock, which prompted an outburst of barking from Jack, as if he were shouting, "Daddy's home, Daddy's home!" Before my husband could get through the door, Jack had barreled through it and begun jumping all over him.

Our dog's loyalty and eagerness to please remind me of how I want to desire God. I want to have a heart for my Master and His powerful, unfailing presence. It is amazing how God's creations, from awe-inspiring landscapes to our little pets, constantly remind us how to worship with adoration. Whatever brings you to worship God today, remain in awe of Him.

LET'S TALK: What about God are you in awe of at this moment? What are some practical ways you can worship Him today and express your adoration?

Faith Laughter

Perfect love casts out fear.
→ 1 John 4:18 (ESV)

Sometimes, fear and panic can really grip us. Have they ever tried to restrain you? Today is a good day to approach fear with a unique twist by responding with "faith laughter." When you feel fear approaching— say, when you open a bill—laugh out loud. At first, you might feel ridiculous or even annoyed. But as unconventional as this approach is, it's a practical way to acknowledge God. It's a reminder of God's perfect love that casts out fear. In this, you're able to see His joy in the midst of trouble.

Think of faith laughter as a holy laughter arising from within us. It's a glorious expression of trust in Him, a joyous deliverance from fear. And take notice of what your children do when they hear you laugh. They laugh, too! God's healing virtues are more contagious than any worries we face. Let your joyful voice declare, sing, and send forth a disruptive vibration of God's perfect love into your family, your home, your community—all the way to God's glorious throne.

LET'S PRAY: "Father God, Your Word declares that I can laugh with no fear of the future because I know that You not only hold my future, You *are* my future. I thank You for today's reminder of who You are, even when circumstances try to convince me otherwise. You are my God. You are Victory. In Jesus's name, amen."

I Found Dirt

So now I am giving you a new
commandment: Love each other.
Just as I have loved you, you should
love each other. → John 13:34

Imagine you decide to start a new career as a gold miner. Your first day on the job, you gather all the necessary equipment and go down into the mines. You begin digging, when suddenly you find dirt—a *lot* of it. Imagine that instead of digging some more, you run out of the cave to share your discovery with your new coworkers, shouting, "I found dirt! I found dirt!"

Doesn't that sound ridiculous? You were hired to be a gold miner, not a dirt miner. Dirt isn't exactly hard to find!

So it is in life with people we know. If you're around a person who's acting inconsiderately or cruelly, it's easy to focus on what's wrong with them. But anyone can see the dirt in people's lives. It takes prayerful intimacy with the Holy Spirit to see what God sees: the treasured gold that is within us all, even when the dirt is so much more evident. His power allows us to discern not only evil but also God's goodness. It's one thing to see the enemy at work in someone's life; it's another level of maturity to know what God intended. When we stay in Christ and see with His eyes, we will be wowed and in awe of God's limitless love.

We have the privilege and honor to call out the gold of God in people. Even when we see the flaws, we also see how God can take His wholeness to their brokenness and make them beautiful.

TRY THIS TODAY: Is there an area in your life where you've been focusing on the dirt when God needed you to see the treasure of who you are in Him? Take that part of yourself to God and ask Him, "Lord, will you show me the treasure of who I am in You?" Pause and close your eyes for a moment. You may get a picture or a word, or perhaps many words that point to scripture. Once you see the treasured gold He placed within you, you'll be able to recognize it in others more easily.

I'm Not Full

For the Kingdom of God is not a matter of what we eat or drink, but of living a life of goodness and peace and joy in the Holy Spirit.
→ Romans 14:17

One night, at dinner with my family, I was eating plenty of food . . . but the more I ate, the more it felt like I hadn't eaten anything. I knew something was going on, but I couldn't quite pinpoint what it was. Then, suddenly, a revelation came: I wasn't feeling satisfied with food because my body was just sensing what my spirit longed for. I had a desperate hunger and thirst for something greater than food—for God's Word, for intimacy with Jesus.

I looked at my husband and said, "Oh my goodness. I'm not hungry for food—it's my spirit crying out for some much-needed time with Jesus." I got up from the table and literally ran to be alone with the Lord. In that moment, I realized that, as today's Bible verse says, the Kingdom of God is really not about what we eat or drink. It's about righteousness, joy, and peace in the Holy Spirit. That time with God was absolutely what I needed. It let me know that God and God alone was the only One who could truly satisfy my soul.

LET'S TALK: Have you been packing your life with needless filler? Replace it with going to God. Watch how He and He alone can fill you.

Beautiful Collision

If I could speak all the languages
of earth and of angels, but didn't love others,
I would only be a noisy gong or a clanging
cymbal. If I had the gift of prophecy, and if I
understood all of God's secret plans and
possessed all knowledge, and if I had such
faith that I could move mountains, but didn't
love others, I would be nothing.
→ 1 Corinthians 13:1–2

God gives us all innate gifts as part of our personalities. We get these gifts whether or not we have a relationship with Him. In fact, it's quite common for people to walk in His gifts without actually knowing Him. For instance, there are people who are generous or organized, people who are great encouragers or who have a natural ability to open up their home to others—yet all the while they have no fellowship with God. Often, people reveal the gifts within them in order to point to themselves and what they do well, rather than to point to God.

But what if we realized that we could operate in the gift that lasts forever—the greatest gift, love? Love is the place from which every gift flows within us by the power of the Holy Spirit. When you go deep enough with Him, His gifts and His love come together in a beautiful collision that points people upward to the Father.

I'll give you an example. Some people have the gift of prophecy, receiving words from God to pass along to others. Not the kind of Old Testament prophecies where God speaks directly through someone, but the kind of prophecies where God puts a message in your heart or mind. If someone with this gift doesn't have the right kind of intimacy with God, the prophetic words they speak might be correct, but they also might be harmful, because they're being interpreted or presented in the wrong way. This person might have intuition about someone else's struggles but use that discernment to find fault with the person, instead of finding the gold and the treasure of God within them. On the other hand, someone with a prophetic gift properly rooted in love wouldn't focus on the struggles. They'd see the power of God to annihilate the struggles and could prophesy about who that person was meant to be in Christ. In that case, the gift would reveal what God truly intended.

The key is intimacy. Be so intertwined with God that you don't want to do anything outside of Him and His love.

LET'S TALK: Have you been walking in a gift from God without pointing back to Him and His love? You can change that today. Be aware of His love, and let the gift be a melody of God's.

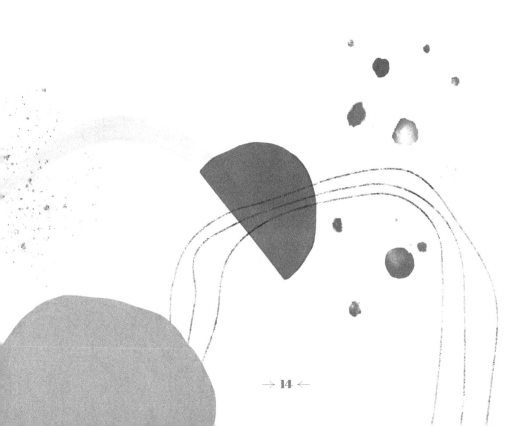

Home Movies

Yet true godliness with contentment is itself great wealth. After all, we brought nothing with us when we came into the world, and we can't take anything with us when we leave it. So if we have enough food and clothing, let us be content. → 1 Timothy 6:6–8

I dusted off the old VCR, plugged it into the entertainment center, and pressed PLAY on some family home videos from 1986. Onscreen, I saw myself in the family room of the house I grew up in, with its ever-so-charming brown shag carpet and paneled walls. My sisters and I were sitting on the floor in front of the artificial Christmas tree, eagerly opening presents from our mom and dad.

Seeing the lack of worries my sisters and I had onscreen, I felt a pleasant sense of nostalgia. We had no idea that the way our parents balanced our lives was evidence of God's grace on our lives. They worked so hard, but as these home movies showed, they enjoyed spending quality time with their children and with each other. When stressful times came, we knew how to laugh in the middle of it all, and we made sure to explore the world, even if it was just our kitchen, backyard, or porch.

Watching the old home movies, I was reminded that in the midst of hard work and the hustle and bustle of life, it's never too late to enjoy your family. Although it's important that our kids see how the bills get paid, we want their greatest memories to be how we had fun together. Moment by moment, when we feel inundated by life, let us turn around and inundate life by enjoying it. Let us reveal our grateful hearts to God and make lasting memories with His creative power!

TRY THIS TODAY: Every day for the next few days, put a simple action in place to enjoy time with your family. Perhaps you can look up a scripture and have each person in your family read it, speak it, and then pray over it together. Depending on the age of your children, perhaps you can assign each child a scripture to read and let them talk about what they learned from God in that scripture.

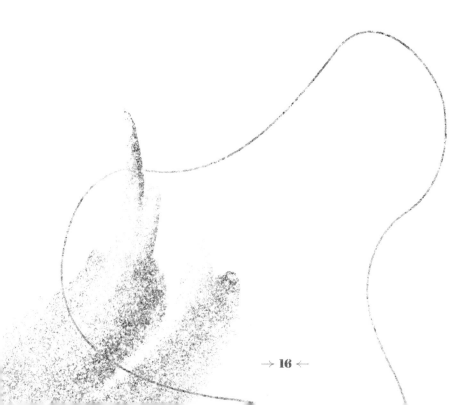

Shine

You are the light of the world— like a city on a hilltop that cannot be hidden. → Matthew 5:14

Think about today's verse. You are the light of the world, like a city set on a hill. And what's the purpose of being set on that hill? The purpose is to shine for all to see! People are watching how we're living. They're observing how we respond to the struggles of life and to the people around us. Are we trying to respond using our own strength? Or are we responding with the Holy Spirit within us and letting God shine through us?

Are we going to God in prayer and leaning in to hear Him? Are we showing His light to everyone around us? Today I want to remind each of us to simply shine! Instead of talking about how dark the world is, let's give the world cause to talk about how bright we are, so that they may glorify our Father God. When we realize who God is, we can't help but just do good to others. It all comes from a place of abundant gratefulness, and it shines through.

TRY THIS TODAY: Ask the Lord how you can practically shine in a situation you're currently facing. Once you get a practical idea for a first step, write it down, take action with the Lord, and watch what unfolds.

Again and Again

Always be full of joy in the Lord.
I say it again—rejoice! → Philippians 4:4

Rejoice. That word has the prefix "re-," which indicates repetition—
to do something over and over. To rejoice is to be joyful again
and again. Rejoicing is not the ability to *act like* you're happy but
rather to be truly full of Jesus, who is our constant joy, no matter
the circumstances.

Our lifestyle of rejoicing points people to the Father God, but how do
we get to that place when the pressures of life seem to surround us?
We're all in different seasons of life; some of us feel overwhelmed
moment to moment, whereas others may feel like we're living the
dream. Either way, true rejoicing is being aware that you're in the Lord
Himself. Think about that. When you receive Jesus as Lord and Savior,
the God of the universe—and universes that haven't even been discovered yet—is within you. That thought alone causes me to be joyful
in the Lord.

TRY THIS TODAY: As you pray, tell the Lord about some of
the times you've seen Him. As you're reminded of them, thank Him
for all He has done, and expect His will for your life. I would even
jot down the date and time when these moments you've recalled
occurred, to help remember all that He has done and stay aware of
the joy He is in our lives.

Shut the Door

Come, let us tell of the Lord's greatness;
let us exalt his name together. I prayed to the
Lord, and he answered me. He freed me from
all my fears. → Psalm 34:3–4

There I was, running 20 minutes late for church, and I just couldn't get my freezer door shut. As I arranged and rearranged the contents, I was tempted to just give up and leave with the freezer door slightly ajar, but I knew that if I just tried a little longer, I could figure out what was obstructing the door. And finally, I did: a can of orange juice. All I had to do was get the source of the problem out of the way, and then I was able to properly shut the freezer.

Sometimes the issues of life are kind of like that can of orange juice. I may unintentionally glorify the problem by letting words of frustration flow out of my mouth. Or I can choose to glorify God in the midst of frustration, focusing on Him instead of the problem. I need to truly observe what I should de-magnify and whom I should magnify.

The can of frozen orange juice reminded me that every day I get to make a choice to praise God, asking Him for wisdom and discernment as He walks me through the obstructions in my life. We need Him as He helps us remove those things that must be removed so we can see and hear Him even more.

Look at today's scripture. When we magnify the Lord as we praise Him, it leads us to seek Him. As we seek Him, He delivers us from all of our fears. On the flip side, when I magnify a problem, it consistently leads me down the path to other problems. What will happen then? It will deliver me into all of my fears. Let's glorify the Lord instead of our problems.

TRY THIS TODAY: Think of an obstruction in your life right now. Then get before the Lord and meditate on today's scripture. Write it out on a notecard if you want to, and think about it throughout the day.

A Time for Everything

For everything there is a season, a time
for every activity under heaven . . .
A time to embrace and a time to turn away.
A time to search and a time to quit searching.
A time to keep and a time to throw away.
→ Ecclesiastes 3:1, 5–6

I had been facilitating an incredible women's group, and I had every intention of continuing to do so. I loved these women, and the way we went after God together was incredible. However, I felt a nudge revealing it was time for this season of my life to end. I wrestled with that nudge. I felt like if I agreed to end it, I was also saying, "I quit."

But then revelation from the Holy Spirit came. I wasn't quitting. I was simply giving back to God what He had originally given to me. Honestly, I still wanted to mourn, because it felt like a huge loss. But again the Holy Spirit ministered to me: "What you give to Me is never lost. Look at all that you have gained in Me. You gained knowing Me." When we see through the eyes of the One who is abundant life, we can see abundance in every season of life, no matter where that season places us.

LET'S PRAY: "Lord, let me be content in You in every season. You are my Hope. You are my God. You are my strength. And even when the seasons change, I praise You, Father, because You never change. In Jesus's name, amen."

Lesson Plan

This is my command—be strong and courageous! Do not be afraid or discouraged. For the Lord your God is with you wherever you go. → Joshua 1:9

A married couple I'm friends with, whom I'll call Jim and Brooke, volunteered to help out at our church's preschool Sunday school class one week. What they didn't realize was that there was no teacher; they'd be the only adults in the classroom. Minutes ticked by as they searched frantically for a lesson plan or anything that would help them manage the job they hadn't realized they'd signed up for.

Suddenly, Jim's searching was interrupted by a sweet little girl's voice. With tear-filled eyes, she said, "Teacher, I need help! I have a snake stuck in my hair!" Puzzled, he said, "What? A snake?" He quickly realized that it was a toy snake. He shook his head, wondering how he'd let his wife talk him into doing this.

As Brooke, oblivious to her husband's plight, tried her best to manage the other kids, Jim carefully pulled one strand of the little girl's hair after another out of the tangle. It seemed to take forever, and when he finally got to the last few strands of hair, he had to break the news to her: "I'm going to have to either cut your hair or cut the snake." The expression on the little girl's face changed instantly, and she cried, "No! Don't cut my snake!" Sweating profusely, he calmed her down and cut just enough hair to free the toy.

A few minutes later, Jim finally found a book filled with Bible lessons for the children. He opened it up and looked at all the helpful activities, but by then it was too late. It was already almost time for the parents to pick up their children. Although it felt like chaos at that point, Jim and Brooke knew to just hang in there—both they and the children would make it out alive, though perhaps with slightly less hair.

To me, this story is a hilarious reminder that many times we don't have any lesson plans to help us prepare for the curveballs of life. Yet we have God's Word and His Spirit to teach us, even when we're unprepared for a challenge. We can trust God to strengthen us and help us, just like it says in today's scripture.

TRY THIS TODAY: There's nothing wrong with feeling irritated or frustrated, like Jim was. But let that annoyance be a notification to press into God. Turn the praise music on and begin to worship Him right where you are.

Finding Grace

Three different times I begged the Lord
to take [the thorn in my flesh] away.
Each time he said, "My grace is all you need."
→ 2 Corinthians 12:8–9

I didn't want to do it. I didn't want to speak to this person about the wrong they'd done. But it was something that the Lord wanted me to walk in with Him. He wanted me to walk in obedience, assisted by His boldness, driven by His love, and I felt convicted to address this issue.

I imagined that with God's help, the conversation would go smoothly, but it was quite the opposite. I immediately regretted that I'd said anything, and my thoughts attempted to carry me away into the pit of despair and depression. I wanted to crawl into bed and ask God to allow me to do the day over again. But then His peace came upon me. I was reminded that the results of obedience are not always what we hope, but we must be obedient anyway. If I got it to do over again, would I disobey God to make my life easier? It wouldn't be worth it.

I may have lost a relationship, but you know what I was able to gain? While addressing what this person had done, I remembered that I had done similar things to others more often than I'd like to admit. That's how I knew my heart was right with God. I wasn't judging this person—I was taking what happened and allowing God to search my own heart.

After this meeting, I was led to make a few phone calls to apologize for misusing God's zeal in the past. It was definitely not something I'd planned to do before that painful conversation. Yet what proof of His love: I received a text that day from a friend who wrote, "Grace. It has been put on my heart to share that word with you. Let me know what God reveals to you. I love you."

LET'S PRAY: Is there an area of your life where you've been avoiding what God has highlighted to you? "Father God, in the name of Jesus, by the power of the Holy Spirit, I need Your help. I surrender my heart to You in this situation. Show me where I have fallen short so I can see how You want to make it right. Thank You, Lord, for Your great help in my time of need. In Jesus's name, amen."

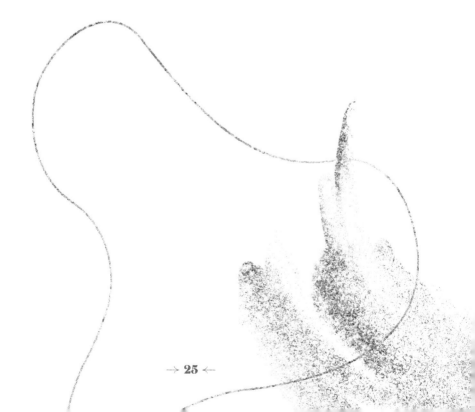

I Can Do It

I can do all things through Christ who strengthens me. → Philippians 4:13 (NKJV)

As soon as she could walk, my daughter, Tristin, would jump into everyday moments, eager to prove she was grown up like we were. Whether it was her version of sweeping, putting dishes away, or making the bed, I could count on that little girl to contribute in some way or another. One time, her grandma, who had been visiting for the week, placed a cup of coffee in the microwave. When the microwave beeped, four-year-old Tristin ran to grab the mug for her grandma. Her grandma warned, "Oh no, Tristin! You can't do that, it's too hot!" That was when Tristin replied, "Grandma, I can do all things through Christ."

It's a moment we still giggle about many years later. She had such confidence that she could truly do all things through Christ. It was profound and yet simply practical to her. Her innate faith in Jesus was so pure and sacred. It's a precious reminder to live out this beautiful, profound truth in my own life.

LET'S TALK: Today, do you want to live knowing who Christ truly is, so that you know you can do all the things He has called you to do in Him? Go to Him right now and really dialogue with Him about what He wants to do through you.

A Recipe for God's Love

In a wealthy home . . . expensive utensils are used for special occasions, and the cheap ones are for everyday use. If you keep yourself pure, you will be a special utensil for honorable use. Your life will be clean, and you will be made ready for the Master to use you for every good work.
→ 2 Timothy 2:20–21

I had everything I needed to make dinner: the necessary utensils, the recipe, the ingredients measured out—and a family with a healthy appetite.

As I cooked, I thought of the parallels between preparing a meal and being prepared in the Lord. He gives us a beautiful recipe for a life guided by the Holy Spirit through the Word of God. When we really read His Word, it lays out the instructions necessary to live not just a good life but a life that reveals whom we belong to and causes us to point others to God. His Holy Spirit prepares us to be set apart and ready for every good work, knowing that we are the salt of the earth and can overcome evil with good. We marinate in God's love and pass through the fire so that others can experience what it means to "taste and see that the Lord is good" (Psalm 34:8).

LET'S PRAY: "Father God, thank You for allowing me to be prepared in You and Your love. Holy Spirit, You are my teacher as I read the Word. I am so grateful that You produce the fruit of the Spirit to reveal Yourself to the world. In Jesus's name, amen."

Corrupt Communication

Let no corrupt communication
proceed out of your mouth, but that which
is good to the use of edifying, that it may
minister grace unto the hearers.
→ Ephesians 4:29 (KJV)

Once, a friend said some things to me that I found so hurtful, I actually went to my room and cried. I attempted to praise God, but the offense I'd received placed a gagging object in my mouth. I felt paralyzed and powerless. I was tempted to call her up and tell her all the most hurtful things I could think of so she'd know how I felt.

While I was crying, having my pity party, one of the scriptures that came up in my spirit was Ephesians 4:29—today's verse. At that moment, I could hear the Spirit say, "You can ask, 'Why?' or you can ask, 'What can I learn from this?'" I remember breathing in and out slowly and leading my mind to the Word instead of the offense.

I shared with a different dear friend what had happened and the scripture I received. She pointed out that Ephesians 4:29 lists two opposite types of communication. On one side, there is "corrupt communication." On the other side, there is communication that is "edifying" and "ministers grace" to people. When we use corrupt com-munication, which is not edifying, we're not ministering grace—we're administering bondage.

Through this point my friend so wisely shared, I learned from the Holy Spirit that His ways are always better. No matter how offended or hurt we feel, we can't resort to harmful words ourselves. If the things we say aren't revealing the grace of God, then are they really worth saying?

LET'S PRAY: "Lord, thank You for Your reminders for me to walk on the path following You. I choose to be someone who ministers grace to the hearers, not bondage. If I love You with Your love, it will be shown through my words and my deeds. Thank You for equipping me by Your Spirit to be a minister of Your grace to all who hear me; allow them to hear You. In Jesus's name, amen."

Eternal Access

So let us come boldly to the throne
of our gracious God. There we will receive his
mercy, and we will find grace to help us when
we need it most. → Hebrews 4:16

A few years ago, my computer screen suddenly turned black.
I assumed the battery must have died, but when I looked, the computer was still plugged in. I laid hands on it and prayed. I took the battery out and put it back in. Nothing helped. A computer tech advised ordering a replacement part, but when it arrived, it didn't fix anything. The tech finally pronounced the computer dead. This couldn't be happening!

That's when I realized how much I relied on that device. It led me to think about what we consider basic necessities, even when they might just be things we want. I'm partial to the saying "God turns our messes into a powerful message." My reaction to the death of my laptop let me know that God wasn't my world the way I thought He was. If you need a reminder like I did, here it is: Long for God more than anything else. Whether or not we have access to our digital files, we always have access to Him, no matter what.

LET'S TALK: Do you want to receive His mercy and find His grace when you need it most? If so, remember that it's found in Him. He wants you to approach His throne with boldness—not out of arrogance but with the knowledge of His love for you.

JOY: Jesus Over You

The joy of the Lord is your strength!
→ Nehemiah 8:10

For many years, I've made wooden signs with life-giving phrases or words hand-painted on them. About 10 years ago, I received this great Holy Spirit idea to paint a wooden spoon rather than a sign, as a reminder to "stir up" the gifts of God within me and others. So I painted a wooden spoon with the word "JOY."

I'd been having a bad day, but I grabbed the freshly painted JOY spoon and started doing a sort of spoon-stirring dance. Still annoyed about my day, I shouted with irritation, "I have the joy of the Lord, which is my strength! Come on, joy!" As I did this silly dance, that joy began to bubble up, and then, instantaneously, irritation became laughter.

The transforming power of God's strength as revealed in His joy never fails. To me, it always feels like a babbling brook inside me. It makes me proclaim my thanks to our God as I worship Him throughout the day by singing, lending a hand, giving someone a word of encouragement, or doing whatever else He leads me to do.

That day, our daughter, Tristin, who was then 12, arrived home notably sad. I embraced her, allowing her to cry and reveal her inner battles. As I gently pulled away, I had an idea. I grabbed my spoon and began to do the same silly dance with the stirring motion I'd done earlier. Dramatically holding the spoon up to my mouth like a microphone, I attempted to sing, which only made it funnier to my daughter.

Then, with a singing shout, I declared, "J-O-Y! Do you know what that stands for?"

Tristin laughed. "What?"

"Jesus Over You!" I knew right then and there that this was by the Holy Spirit of God! We laughed as I took her by the hand and we started running through the house. Our giggles became weapons against sadness. Remember, the joy of the Lord is your strength! Let it pull you out of your pit of despair.

TRY THIS TODAY: Stir up joy! I even challenge you to physically grab a spoon and stir it up. Be aware of Jesus Over You and let Him be revealed in you today!

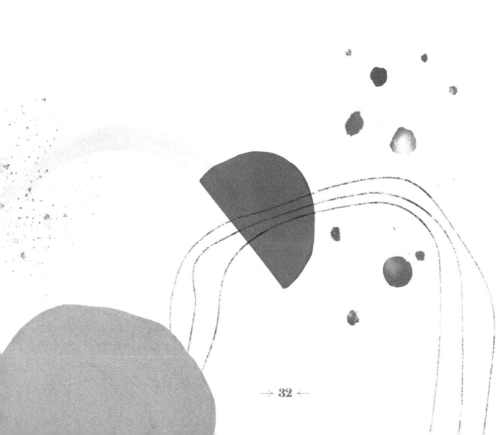

Just Ask

If you need wisdom, ask our generous God, and he will give it to you. He will not rebuke you for asking. But when you ask him, be sure that your faith is in God alone. → James 1:5–6

Have you ever been in a situation where you wanted to pray about something, but you felt it was too insignificant to ask God for help? A moment when you needed wisdom to navigate a situation that might seem minor to others but feels major to you? I definitely have.

Today's scripture is a powerful reminder not to believe the lie that you can't ask for God's help in small matters. God is generous. He won't scold you for asking for wisdom; He'll honor and esteem you. He'll give it to you in a way that shows He's so glad you asked. He desires for us to see Him in the way He intended, to come to Him from a place of knowing how much He loves us. Have you been hesitant to ask God for wisdom in your life? Do you want to stop that at this moment? Just ask Him. He's waiting to answer you in ways you have not imagined.

TRY THIS TODAY: Find one or two scriptures that speak of God's wisdom. (Feel free to search online!) Write them down, or type them into the notes app on your phone. Once you have them, pray for God's wisdom and understanding over yourself. No matter the situation, expect that He will show you things you never imagined.

Love My Enemies?

I say, love your enemies! Pray for those who persecute you! In that way, you will be acting as true children of your Father in heaven.
→ Matthew 5:44–45

There have been a few times when the words of this scripture have come up speedily in my spirit, especially when I feel like anyone is messing with my children or family. Have you had moments when you can imagine doing major harm to someone? As much as they've upset me, that scripture always swoops in by the Spirit of God and saves me (and saves my enemies from me!).

There's a message in today's scripture: God longs to get His love to our enemies through us. Praying over those who have hurt or persecuted us reveals our faith and trust in the divine nature of God; it is the "how" in loving our enemies. He wants us to sow blessings, even though it's in our nature to do the opposite.

TRY THIS TODAY: When you read today's scripture, did you automatically think of someone who hurt you? Write their name down, place your hand on the paper, and pray: "Jesus! I partner with You to say, 'Father, forgive them for they know not what they have done.' Show me what You intended for their life. I no longer want to be hurt *by* people; I want to hurt *for* them, feeling their pain along with them. In Jesus's name, amen."

Immovable Yet Moving

Bless the Lord who is my immovable Rock.
→ Psalm 144:1 (TLB)

I remember hearing my children screaming with glee, then walking into the living room to find they'd turned my prized space into a giant pillow fort. You may be thinking, *How sweet!* I thought, *How inconsiderate!* Instead of seeing the fun in their efforts, I saw a mess.

As today's scripture points out, the Lord is our immovable Rock. Circumstances don't move Him the way they moved me that day—and yet He is constantly moving in ways we could never imagine. He goes before us, a countless number of steps ahead, yet remains nearer than near. As we pray, He is not catching up to us; we are catching up to Him and what He has planned for us.

I wish I could say that I joined my kids in their adventurous efforts at a pillow fort. Sadly, that wasn't the case. If I could speak to my younger self, I'd tell her to not be moved. I can't do that, but if you're a mom with young kids, I can urge you to try to stand firm through the situations that seem inconvenient or irritating.

LET'S TALK: How can you see an irritating situation as an opportunity to learn about what's inside of you that God wants to replace with Himself? Write down one to three things that you can look back on to see how God was immovable, even when you were moved. Then thank the Lord for His steadfast love in the midst of shakable times.

Grace to Trust

Trust in the Lord with all your heart;
do not depend on your own understanding.
Seek his will in all you do, and he will show you
which path to take. → Proverbs 3:5–6

Growing up, wherever we lived, we had a basketball hoop in our driveway with Proverbs 3:5 etched in the cement. The same verse was placed on the walls of our home and on any card that was ever signed by my parents. It was a reminder to trust God with *all* of our hearts.

I had to keep that verse in mind many years ago when our family dog at the time (not Jack, whom I wrote about in an earlier devotion) attacked our daughter, Tristin, who was then two years old. He grabbed her face with his teeth and shook her like a rag doll. I screamed, and it felt like I flew in to grab her in slow motion. In that moment, I was faced with a question: "Will I trust You, Lord, even in this?"

I held Tristin in my arms and ran out the front door screaming, "Help us!" I was looking for any neighbor who would be willing to help us, because we had just moved into the neighborhood and had no idea where the nearest hospital was. Praise God, a neighbor heard me and went into action mode. She calmed us both down and helped me with directions to the nearest urgent care. The bite was so bad that once we got to urgent care, they sent us to the emergency room.

In those moments, even as my heart trembled in fear, God's trust-worthy love surrounded us, and I felt a rare peace. Although I was so scared for my daughter, God revealed that He wasn't scared—He was carrying us. Looking back, I even remember that as we drove to the emergency room, my daughter pointed to the side of her face that hadn't been bitten and sweetly said, "Mommy, dis side okay." I just know the Holy Spirit was comforting her in the midst of the chaos. He will comfort you, too.

LET'S PRAY: "Father God, I trust You have gone before me. Even when I'm caught off guard, none of this has caught You by surprise. Although I may be scared, You are not. You are my help in time of need, and I need You more than anyone or anything else. Open my eyes so I can see You right now in the midst of chaos. In Jesus's name, amen."

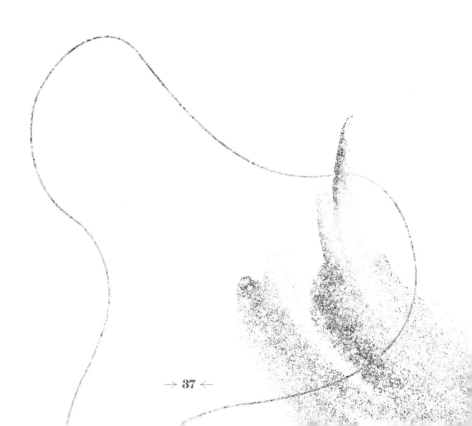

Pain before Victory

God blesses those who patiently endure testing and temptation. Afterward they will receive the crown of life that God has promised to those who love him. → James 1:12

I have often asked, "Why is victory so often preceded by pain?" Trained soldiers die in combat to win a war. A woman has labor pains right before the beautiful birth of her baby. Jesus died as He paid in full our debts of sin. Yet as we go through the pain, we are not alone.

When do you need strength the most? When you're weak. So joy shall be supplied with endless power, especially when you feel depression enter. Human happiness is determined by our circumstances, but the joy of the Lord gets us through, no matter what's going on in our lives. Personally, I often feel joy at times when it doesn't seem to make sense, especially to the people around me. I walk in joy by faith in God.

You can go through trials with joy as God provides you the strength to get to where you need to go. When we fix our eyes on the provider of our righteousness, peace, strength, and more, that's when we're able to live a life that people will ask about and eventually want to experience. May we find strength in Jesus Christ as He gives us unspeakable joy and perfect peace that surpasses all understanding.

LET'S TALK: Where do you need joy to be revealed in your life today? Will you write that down and find scriptures about joy and/or the issue you're struggling with?

Pizza Delivery

Do to others whatever you would like
them to do to you. This is the essence
of all that is taught in the law and
the prophets. → Matthew 7:12

My daughter, Tristin, and I had had a long day, and it showed in our attitudes. We were trying to have a conversation, but the way we were talking, neither of us was honoring the other. I don't remember why there was an empty pizza box lying around, but when I saw it, I got an idea. It wasn't an idea that immediately made much sense, but I was ready to follow the lead of whatever the Holy Spirit wanted us both to learn.

I interrupted our heated conversation, grabbed the pizza box, and walked out the front door in a dramatic style. Shutting the door behind me, I waited for a few seconds, then rang the doorbell.

Tristin opened the door. "Yes?"

"Pizza delivery," I said, and threw the pizza box in her direction. She looked at me in utter confusion.

I ran to pick up the pizza box and said, "I'm going to do that again." I went back outside, shut the door, and rang the doorbell again.

This time around, she opened the door hesitantly.

"Pizza delivery," I said again, but this time I gently handed the box to her.

It was like a hyperbolic skit that the Holy Spirit was using to teach both of us a lesson. "Which delivery did you like better?" I asked. She said, "The second one." Our delivery is such a huge part of communication. As today's scripture points out, we should communicate with one another in a way that is considerate, treating others the way we would want to be treated.

LET'S PRAY: "Father God, thank You for Your Holy Spirit. I want others to know they are loved when I interact with them, as I would want to feel the same way. Thank You, Father, for even if no one else does it, I get to treat others well because I am doing it for You. In Jesus's name, amen."

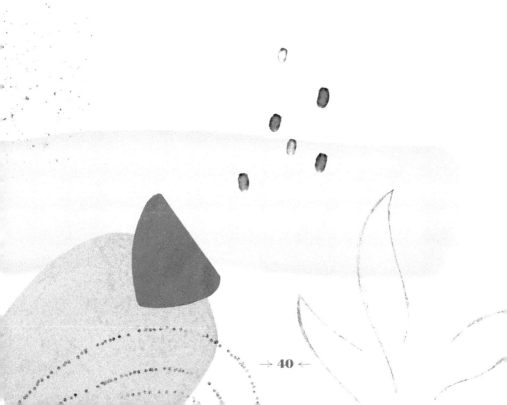

Unconventional

Instead, God chose things the world considers foolish in order to shame those who think they are wise. → 1 Corinthians 1:27

"Remove yourself from Facebook and Instagram." This is what I heard God telling me to do, right when I was in the middle of an Instagram campaign to highlight my YouTube channel. It's a channel that encourages people not only to have good perspective but to have *God's* perspective—to live by the power of God's Word in every situation of our lives. It didn't make sense to remove myself from the social platforms just as I was gaining traction in spreading the gospel this way. Just entertaining the notion felt daunting. I even thought, *This can't be from God*. Yet with every passing day, I felt that prompting to remove myself from social media indefinitely.

When I finally settled it with God that I would obey, I thought of the word "unconventional," meaning not conforming to the way most people act or think. Yes, it was a bit unconventional to be struggling with God about Instagram, but I believe He was highlighting today's scripture. He takes the seemingly foolish things of the world and uses them to teach us lessons we don't expect.

And did He ever! I ended up spending seven months away from social media, and it helped me get closer to God as He taught me how to draw and paint. I'd never even been able to properly draw stick figures, but soon I was drawing and sketching, painting abstracts with acrylics on large canvases, and worshiping all the while.

Have you been feeling a nudge to do something unconventional with God? Maybe it's time to listen.

LET'S PRAY: "Father God, You love it when I step out into the unknown with You. My fears of the unknown are laid at Your feet. Thank You for calling me out into the things that seem foolish yet are the very things that show Your wisdom. In Jesus's name, amen."

Letting Go to Receive

But now I am going away to the
one who sent me, and not one of you is asking
where I am going. Instead, you grieve because
of what I've told you. But in fact, it is best for
you that I go away, because if I don't, the
Advocate won't come. → John 16:5–7

As I read today's scripture, I think of all those times when I dreaded the thought of releasing my daughter into adulthood. It shook me to realize that in order for her to receive the greater things, I would need to release my grip and let her fly. In today's verses, we see that the disciples were distressed that Jesus was leaving them, much like I was distressed at the thought of my daughter leaving me. But Jesus conveys with compassion and authority why He needs to return to His Father in heaven. He did what He was incredibly purposed to do, which was to give His life for the world (John 3:16). He knew His Father's promise was coming. He wasn't seeing this exchange with sadness but with abundant celebration.

From my own human perspective, I can see why the disciples were troubled. Yet I'm also reminded that we are inhabited by the power of the Holy Spirit. That's a compelling nudge to lean into God's divine nature today.

TRY THIS TODAY: I encourage you to write down today's scripture and bask in knowing we have an Advocate called the Holy Spirit. I also encourage you to read the entire chapter of John 16.

From Traps to Safety

Fearing people is a dangerous trap,
but trusting the Lord means safety.
→ Proverbs 29:25

Fearing people comes in many forms: Worrying that someone will hurt you the way you were hurt in the past. Feeling the desire to please people to a fault. It can even come in the form of saying yes to people when you don't want to or shouldn't. This is something I still struggle with.

What I like to do when I read scripture is say, "Holy Spirit, will You be my teacher? Please let me be aware of what You want to say." From my experience, whenever I pray this, I can imagine my child coming to me to learn, which makes me more receptive to what God has to teach me. Now, I don't believe my prayer *causes* the Holy Spirit to suddenly become my teacher. Rather, I believe the prayer stirs awareness in me that He is the Teacher and has been teaching all along—my ears are now simply open to hear Him.

With all that said, let's go back to today's scripture and look at how the Holy Spirit is teaching us. "Fearing people is a dangerous trap, but trusting the Lord means safety." Conversely, when we trust that the Lord is our safety, then we won't fall into the dangerous trap of fearing people. No matter what's going on around us, those difficult moments will attempt to distract us from God. But as we long to stay in Him by reading His Word, we can know that when God says He is for us, it doesn't matter who's against us. We have no need to fear people. Although that seems easier said than done, into eternity it's the truth.

LET'S PRAY: "Father God, thank You for being my safety. As I trust in You, I will avoid the trap of pleasing people over pleasing You. Thank You for keeping me and teaching me as You navigate me through this life. You are my strength and rescuer from every snare as I remain in You and You in me. In Jesus's name, amen."

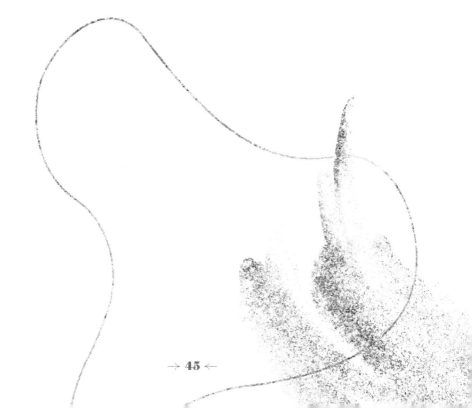

Mustard Seeds

Here is another illustration Jesus used:
"The Kingdom of Heaven is like a mustard
seed planted in a field. It is the smallest of all
seeds, but it becomes the largest of garden
plants; it grows into a tree, and birds come
and make nests in its branches."
→ Matthew 13:31–32

In today's scripture, Jesus gives a hint as to what the Kingdom of
Heaven is like. He specifically references the famous mustard seed.
As I read it, I thought for a moment, *Why compare it to something
so finite? Why not something grandiose?* But it seemed as soon as
that thought came, another pushed it out. It was as though I could
see these words so plainly from 1 Corinthians 1:27 (KJV): "God hath
chosen the foolish things of the world to confound the wise."

Think about this with great awe and wonder. Although the mustard
seed is the smallest of all seeds, it becomes the largest of garden
plants. What's inside the seed is not constrained by what it was con-
tained by; it just grows as God intended and created it to.

It leads me to think about moments of growth in our lives. Have we
allowed fears, past or present hurts, how we were (or weren't) raised,
tragedies, the unknown, health problems, or unfulfilled dreams to tell
us how far we can go in this life? Are we allowing those things to
contain our capacity? Or do we grow into who we were meant to be
because we believe in God and what He has placed within us?

LET'S TALK: What does today's devotion stir you to recognize? Do you see how God is reminding you of who He is versus who you think you are? You are not your past. You are not what others said you were. Is there a lie you believed about who you are that you can give up to God today? As you go to Him, write down how He encourages you stay in Him today.

Yeast

Jesus also used this illustration:
"The Kingdom of Heaven is like the yeast a
woman used in making bread. Even though
she put only a little yeast in three measures
of flour, it permeated every part of the dough."
→ Matthew 13:33

In today's scripture, Jesus uses another illustration explaining the Kingdom of Heaven. Just as He compared the Kingdom to the mustard seed, now He compares it to yeast. They are both so small, yet the end result of what they're purposed to do is big.

The ratio of yeast to flour doesn't make sense at first glance. How could such a small amount of yeast have such a huge impact on all that flour? For a moment, let's think of that flour as a symbol of all that we think we are, all that we have or haven't done, all that we have or don't have. Then just one drop of Jesus's blood comes in and makes us into something we could never have imagined.

It reminds me that all our efforts and accolades are squashed into nothing compared to this grace from God. It might seem far away at times, but it's incredibly tangible, especially when we look back and see how God's grace permeated us when we thought we were on our own.

LET'S PRAY: "Lord, thank You, for even the tiniest bit of Your grace transforms my entire being, overwhelming my efforts as You cause my mere success to be so significant in You. In Jesus's name, amen."

Children and Infants

O Lord, our Lord, your majestic name
fills the earth! Your glory is higher than the
heavens. You have taught children and infants
to tell of your strength, silencing your enemies
and all who oppose you. → Psalm 8:1–2

I used to overlook the sound of a child singing or a baby cooing, allowing it to be background noise—until I read today's scripture. After I read through it, I stopped and read it again. Think about this. God has taught children and infants to tell of His strength, and it doesn't stop there. There's a purpose to His teaching them. Did you catch it? God has taught them for the purpose of *silencing the enemies*.

As soon as I realized this, I wanted to embrace every baby and child I saw. I've never been one to get "baby fever" around kids who aren't mine, but when I read about how God taught them to praise Him, it changed everything. These children are so precious and pure, and their innocence is taken from them more often than I'd like to imagine. There are so many adults who struggle because they were preyed upon by the enemy when they were young.

Isn't it amazing that children often have more understanding of God than adults? They don't have to attend a Bible college or a theology class. They simply know Him. We could attempt to teach them on any level, and they would somehow get it, because their spirits are responding to God Himself. Jesus said in Matthew 18:3 that unless you come to the Father as a child, you won't enter the Kingdom of Heaven. Now that is a statement right there.

TRY THIS TODAY: If you have a baby or toddler, call out their name and tell them, "I know who you are! You are a son/daughter of God, aren't you? You, my son, are like a well-nurtured plant, and you, my daughter, are as a graceful pillar, carved to beautify a palace (Psalm 144:12). Everywhere you go, you make it better because of Jesus." Watch how they respond. It's incredible. Write down scriptures today that you can declare over your child(ren), especially when you're having a hard time with them. That's the time to really proclaim who they are!

Sold Out

The Kingdom of Heaven is like a treasure that a man discovered hidden in a field. In his excitement, he hid it again and sold everything he owned to get enough money to buy the field. → Matthew 13:44

I have to step back and admire the man in this parable. He discovered hidden treasure in a field, and excitement stirred. But did he take the treasure home? No! Instead, he reburied it. After that, did he go home and resume his life as usual? No! He went back home to sell everything so he could buy the land that housed the treasure.

This story opens my eyes to see Jesus. He saw us as God's treasure within the earth. He went back to His rightful home of heaven and sold it all for each of us. Jesus did this for you and me. And He set the example for how we bring the Kingdom to our world. We see people as the treasure, we return to God, and we surrender it all. We recognize the value in giving all we are to God, because in return, we'll see the treasures He buried within people. Giving it all up is worth it so that we can receive new life in Him and follow after Him as He intended.

LET'S PRAY: "Father God, thank You for being the greatest treasure, and thank You for seeing me as a treasure and selling everything to purchase me. You paid with Your life. In Jesus's name, amen."

Submission Is Resistance

Submit to God. Resist the devil and he will flee from you. → James 4:7 (NKJV)

For years I found myself exhausted spiritually. I thought, *Why do the scriptures say to "always be joyful"?* It felt like I was spending all my time fighting against the devil but never stopping to appreciate God's love. Without realizing it, I was pushing away my family and God. I was slowly getting miserable.

Until, one day, something changed. The only way I can explain it is that there was a voice in my spirit. Not literally—it was more like I suddenly had a clear understanding. The voice said, "Are you tired of resisting the enemy? A better way to resist the enemy is by submitting to Me."

I laugh as I remember it, but at the time, it was like a bucket of cold water to my face. It was one of those aha moments that help us really understand that the Holy Spirit knows all things. This newfound revelation highlighted God's grace that abounds when we submit to Him. That moment is when I realized this is how we draw near to God—not by trying to resist the enemy with our own strength but by giving in and yielding to God. Submission *is* resistance.

LET'S TALK: Have you exhausted yourself trying to resist the enemy? Now that you understand that giving in to God is what lets us resist the enemy, how you can submit to God right now?

Behavior Follows Transformation

Let the message about Christ, in all its richness, fill your lives. Teach and counsel each other with all the wisdom he gives. Sing psalms and hymns and spiritual songs to God with thankful hearts. And whatever you do or say, do it as a representative of the Lord Jesus, giving thanks through him to God the Father. → Colossians 3:16–17

A huge lesson I've learned in the Lord is that behavior follows transformation. When we are transformed by God, our behavior follows the Spirit of God. We experience a desire to partner with the Holy Spirit within us, and we begin demonstrating who He is by our actions. We become "representatives of the Lord Jesus," as today's scripture puts it. When we understand this concept, we can be more patient with people when their behaviors aren't what we might hope they'd be—and we can pray that God and His love will transform them, which will in turn change their behavior as well.

Remember, the telltale sign of someone's spiritual maturity is not necessarily that they can recite tons of scripture, lead with influence, write well, or speak prophetically. The transformed don't have to be the scholarly ones or the ones who show up to church every time the doors are open. They are simply ones who are known by God's love and mark others for God's glory in such a way that they're never the same. God's goodness is where the miracles of transformation are seen.

TRY THIS TODAY: Think about someone you've "tried" to be nice to, and write their name down in a journal or in the notes app on your phone. Place your hand over their name and say, "Lord, I give this person over to You. I need Your love to pray for them. Cover them and keep them safe. Open their ears and eyes to hear and see You, and open their heart to receive what You want to give to them." Now, as you're led by the Holy Spirit, ask God to highlight a scripture that you can declare over them today. Expect His love to transform your heart toward them.

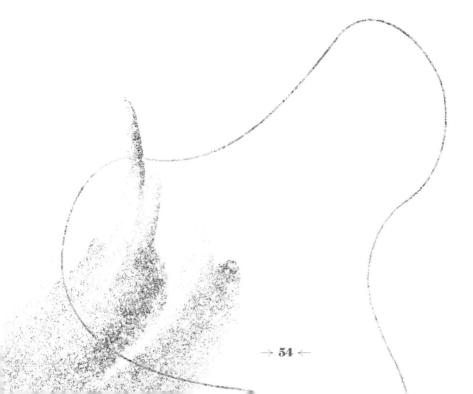

The Night Sky

When I look at the night sky and see the work of your fingers—the moon and the stars you set in place—what are mere mortals that you should think about them, human beings that you should care for them? Yet you made them only a little lower than God and crowned them with glory and honor. → Psalm 8:3–5

As I think about the glorious night sky and how it displays the glory of God's masterful touch, it leads me to think, "How can we ever be distracted by the petty things of this life?" The words of Psalm 8, written millennia ago by King David, clear out selfish pride so that you can't help but be humbled by His majesty. God's creation helps us become "divinely distracted" by the glory of God.

Today, let His glorious power hush your racing thoughts, your fears of the unknown, and your embittered moments of offense. Forsake it all in full surrender to our amazing God. If He can make the moon and the stars, you can trust Him with your life's circumstances.

LET'S PRAY: "Father God, I want to be more in awe of You than of any distraction of this world. Any hurts or disappointments don't come close to Your power. Lord, I know there is nothing too difficult for You. Your faithful promises are even seen through the evidence of creation. May my life be one that displays Your glorious majesty. In Jesus's name, amen."

The Joy of Integrity

Joyful are people of integrity, who follow the instructions of the Lord. → Psalm 119:1

Those who have integrity are joyful. That's a simple truth, isn't it? But let's also think about the flip side. When we don't have integrity, we don't have joy. We feel shame, even depression, and the weight of guilt, because we cut corners or weren't fully transparent. There's no relief.

Once, I got back from a shopping trip and found an item I hadn't purchased in my bag. I had those wrestling thoughts: "I'm already home . . . no one would notice . . ." Yet I just knew I had to return it. It would have been convenient for me to keep this item I hadn't paid for, but it wouldn't bring me the feeling of joy I got when I brought it back, knowing that I not only did something that pleased God, but I also got to minister to the store's employees by setting a good example. The pleasure of knowing that we get to help bring others to God is far more profound than getting a free item could ever be.

LET'S PRAY: "Father, thank You for the power of Your Holy Spirit that lives within me and gives me a life of joy. Being in awe of You allows me to want to do what is pleasing to You, which causes joy to stir. Thank You for the power to live in constant joy. In Jesus's name, amen."

You Can't Unread

This means that anyone who belongs to Christ has become a new person. The old life is gone; a new life has begun! → 2 Corinthians 5:17

My daughter and I were sitting on the couch, wrapped in fluffy blankets as we reminisced about when she was little. I was telling her how, before she could read, she would often open up her little books and just make up her own storylines. We laughed as I imitated how she wouldn't skip a beat. Anyone watching her would have thought for sure that she was reading every word on the page.

We began talking about how we couldn't remember what it was like to *not* be able to read. We even attempted to imagine "unreading"—the idea of not knowing how to read once you learn how—but it was truly unfathomable, at least to us. We shook our heads, giggling because we couldn't really comprehend such a thought.

Similarly, the revelation of God's Word transforms our minds and our thinking so deeply that to attempt to think in the same ways we used to is hilariously daunting. We might vaguely remember how we used to see the world, but we can't fully imagine how we went through life with that kind of mindset. Once we begin to see the way God sees as He reveals Himself to us, it's just impossible to "unread" His ways!

LET'S TALK: Have you experienced this as well? Do you ever step back in awe of how your mindset has changed and transformed? Really think about the miracle-working power of God that you have experienced. We don't read the Word just to get more knowledge but to be transformed by it—to live out His presence in our everyday moments and reveal His lovingkindness, which is a miracle in and of itself.

The Exception to the Rule

Don't rejoice when your enemies fall; don't be happy when they stumble. For the Lord will be displeased with you and will turn his anger away from them. → Proverbs 24:17–18

The Bible usually tells us to be joyful, but this verse gives us an exception to the rule. The only time we're not supposed to rejoice is when our enemies fall and stumble. As I read this, a revelatory thought came to my spirit: "Your rejoicing is an instrument of praise. It helps set your gaze on Me, your God. When you use the tool of rejoicing to laugh at the enemy, it reveals that your focus has not been on Me and that you have been seduced away from the awareness of My presence yet again."

We can celebrate and be joyful because of the goodness and faithfulness of God. He is the reason for our laughter. If the Lord would be displeased by us rejoicing at an enemy falling, then a great way to please and align with Him would be to pray what He would want us to pray over them. When you do, you get to partner with God in reconciling a soul back to Himself. How amazing would it be to be a part of that miracle?

TRY THIS TODAY: Write down five things that cause you to be in awe of the Lord. Then worship Him and thank Him for all that He is and has done. In His presence, what did He reveal to you about what He wants to do for your enemies?

The Final Conclusion

Fear God and obey his commands,
for this is everyone's duty. God will judge us for
everything we do, including every secret thing,
whether good or bad. → Ecclesiastes 12:13–14

The book of Ecclesiastes reveals Solomon's wavering thoughts as he assesses the meaning of this life. When I read this book, I feel like a witness to his angst—all the tormented thoughts that he reveals when he writes about experiences that left him to wonder, *All of this—for what?* As a reader, you can almost tangibly sense his frustration with the many decisions he has made or not made throughout his life.

Yet despite the pain of everything he writes about, it's all eventually settled. In the end, he sees that the fear of the Lord is the beginning of wisdom. After everything he's written in the entire book of Ecclesiastes, it seems like he's saying, "All of what I just wrote was complicated and sometimes confusing, so just remember this one simple thing: Fear God and obey Him." That's his final conclusion.

LET'S TALK: Where are your affections? Have they been on things that have no eternal value? Are they in God and God alone? These questions don't condemn us but bring light to the hidden places that need to be surrendered to the Father as He waits so patiently. What is He showing you right now?

Discomfort

Let us think of ways to motivate one
another to acts of love and good works.
→ Hebrews 10:24

The call to persevere and motivate in Hebrews 10:24 sounds so
inspiring and incredible—until someone hurts us. At least, that's how
it is for me. We all have different ways of getting motivated, but trials
quickly demotivate most of us, and we return to being selfish. In some
ways, that's what's most comfortable. But in other ways, it's not; I'm
amazed at the ways God can make my flesh squirm when I don't do
what He wants me to do. But if we think about it, this discomfort is
actually a good thing. It motivates us to do what God wants, which is
loving others with our good works. This is an active way to destroy the
works of the flesh and replace them with the works of the Spirit.

A subtle lie attempts to convince us that whatever annoyance or
wound we're holding so dear is more important than anyone or anything else. It causes us to think of ways to *not* be loving, to *not* reveal
the good works that point to the Father. But whatever it is that we're
holding on to, it's temporary, fleeting, and has no eternal value. The
Kingdom of God actually cheers that it happened, because the Kingdom doesn't think about what we might have lost—it thinks of what
we gain by sowing seeds of love and good works!

All the temporal, monetary, or otherwise earthly things I've held so
close and considered so dear just can't be more important than my
relationship with God and my relationships with people. In the scope
of eternity, moments of pain and discomfort can be indicators to set
our gaze back on our Almighty God. This not only motivates us but
also reminds us of the great mandate to think of ways to motivate
one another.

LET'S TALK: When you have a few moments, read Hebrews 10:19–39. What are some things that stand out to you? How can they help you see with an eternal perspective instead of an earthly one?

Victorious Right Hand

Don't be afraid, for I am with you.
Don't be discouraged, for I am your God. I will
strengthen you and help you. I will hold you up
with my victorious right hand. → Isaiah 41:10

Reading today's scripture, I remember how fearful we would be without God. What would our lives look like without the great encouragement from the Lord we get through verses like this one? We would be so frightened and discouraged if God were not with us. And without Him, we would not be strengthened or helped. We would be crushed by defeat. But in reality, we are blessed by the Lord and His steadfast promise that He is with us, so there is no reason to be afraid. His power for us is greater than anything that could be against us.

Additionally, the last sentence in Isaiah 41:10 says, "I will hold you up with my victorious right hand." Think about how exciting that is. Who sits at the right hand of the Father, according to Mark 16:19? It's Jesus! Jesus is the victorious right hand of God who upholds you, the One who elevates you. Wow—what a promise!

LET'S PRAY: "Thank You, Father God, for Your promise that I never need to be afraid, for You are with me. No matter what it looks like around me, the one thing that remains is You. Thank You for Jesus, who upholds and elevates me. I make myself aware of Your goodness today. In Jesus's name, amen."

Get Sharp

As iron sharpens iron, so a friend sharpens a friend. → Proverbs 27:17

How often have you heard the phrase "I'm your parent, not your friend"? After saying this a few years ago, I was quickly convicted by my words. After all, God wants to be my friend, so why wouldn't I want to be my child's?

That question got me thinking about what a friend should be. I came to the conclusion that it's someone who wants the best for you. A friend wants you to be happy, but not in ways that are bad for you in the long term. That's why they tell you the truth, whether it's easy to hear or not. As today's verse puts it, a friend "sharpens" you and brings out the best in you. I ended up realizing that I was raising one of my best friends, in that I want the best for my child. God wants the best for us, too. He was a friend to us first, so that we could be a friend to Him and then to others. In this exchange, He sharpens us and reveals how to be a proper friend so that we can point others forward and upward to Him. We must learn how to be a proper friend to others, especially our children.

LET'S TALK: How has the Lord sharpened you to be more like Him recently? Write it down and reflect on His friendship and His goodness. Then write down how you can help sharpen one of your friends in turn.

Every Word

Every word of God proves true.
He is a shield to all who come to him
for protection. → Proverbs 30:5

God is truth and doesn't have the ability to lie. In the truth of who He is, it's amazing how He sees Himself as a shield for those who believe that He is their protection. Just think on that. He doesn't just give us protection; He is protection itself.

Yet whether He shields us is contingent upon whether we come to Him. When I come to Him, I stop, pause, and say, "Father, I come to You. My awareness is now on You. I'm aware of You, Lord, to yield to hearing Your voice."

He has done His part. He is ready with His arms open wide. He bids us to come to Him and woos us to the Father's heart.

LET'S PRAY: "Father God, thank You for being my shield and protector. Thank You for inviting me to come to You. So here I am, Lord. Thank You that Your Word proves true. I am Yours, and You are mine. In Jesus's name, amen."

The Blessed Way of Living

God blesses you when people mock you and persecute you and lie about you and say all sorts of evil things against you because you are my followers. Be happy about it!
→ Matthew 5:11–12

Whenever I've thought of living a blessed life, it has always been with a mindset of operating in the gifts of God or living a life of plenty and material abundance. Yet today's scripture shows the rawness of a blessed life. It's definitely not of this world—and that's how you really know it has to be of God.

I am in awe that the evidence of living the blessed life is not ease and comfort but rather being mocked, persecuted, lied about, and gossiped about for following after Jesus. Now, of course, this does not refer to being mocked because we're being rude to those who don't follow Jesus; it's talking about when we reveal God's lovingkindness and are still persecuted. It's amazing, this radical love Jesus walks in when He takes it a step further and says, "Don't just tolerate the persecution. Be happy about it!"

This concept definitely rattles the mind. It's almost incomprehensible. It's a cause for reevaluation. Persecution would not be my definition of "blessed," but it is God's, because everything about it directs people to the Father God and how good He is. What a blessing to be a sign that points to Him over and over again.

LET'S PRAY: "Thank You, Lord, for showing me how to live this life in You, which is the only way to live. Lord, I want to follow after You, with Your love that is unoffendable and enlarges my heart for those who attempt to hurt me. Father, I no longer want to be hurt by people; I now want Your heart so I hurt *for* them. In Jesus's name, amen."

It Doesn't Get Better Than This

I could have no greater joy than to hear
that my children are following the truth.
→ 3 John 4

As I meditate on today's scripture, I think about the way it shows just how wonderful it is to hear, know, and witness that our children are following the truth—not just the abstract concept of the truth, but the God who is truth.

There's something so joyous about seeing the next generation carrying on the legacy of Jesus. One thing I've learned in parenting is that I'm not raising children; I'm raising leaders who are following the greatest Leader of all, and His name is Jesus.

When we go about our daily lives with this kind of intentionality, we are able to press past the unpredictable moments of life, especially with our young ones, surrendering our children daily to the Lord, declaring they will follow after Jesus with God's fiery passion all the days of their lives.

LET'S PRAY: "Father, thank You for the gift of who You are as truth. I pray that my child(ren) will follow after You; this is the joy I want to experience all the days of my life, the joy of knowing they follow You. Lord, You are so good and powerful that You want this for them even more than I could want it for them. In Jesus's name, amen."

The Compassion of Christ

One day as he saw the crowds gathering, Jesus went up on the mountainside and sat down. His disciples gathered around him, and he began to teach them. → Matthew 5:1–2

It's amazing to see the mission of God's heart through the unfolding of Jesus's journey as recorded in Matthew 5. Jesus presented the Kingdom of God through parables, drawing analogies from wherever He was at any given moment and telling spirit-provoking stories that tore down the walls within the soul. Before He performed any miracles, signs, or wonders, he told stories with compassion.

Think about this. Jesus was led by God's love into the world, giving up His right to be God due to the compassion of God that compelled Him. Compassion fueled Him as He went into the world, anchored by the love of the Father.

This shows us how compassion and humility go hand in hand. A life of humility allows compassion to rest on us, causing God's power to be revealed in the most improbable ways. Humility strips off the old, shifting from a mindset that says, "How dare they?" to a mindset that says, "How dare I try to get in the way of God's love for them?"

Defaulting to prideful, self-serving ways seems so automatic, doesn't it? (It does to me, at least!) And yet as we read Matthew 5, we see that Jesus is so compassionate. He sits His disciples down and has this heart-to-heart with them—which is the Father's heart to their hearts. No matter what, He is there to teach them and love them.

LET'S TALK: Read Matthew 5. What is one thing that sticks out to you about what Jesus taught that day? With that one thing in mind, how can you practically demonstrate your trust in the Lord's compassion? When you have a moment, journal your insights or share them with someone else.

Opportunities to Praise

Even though the fig trees have no blossoms,
and there are no grapes on the vines . . .
yet I will rejoice in the Lord!
→ Habakkuk 3:17–18

The bed seemed to whisper, "Just crawl under the sheets for a month, let your son take care of your daughter, and everything will be okay." A lying spirit of despair seemed to rise over me. I was feeling this deep sadness because my husband was going to be away on business for over 30 days. Yet in the same moment, that still, small voice spoke so loudly that it rescued me from the lie. The life-changing whisper said, "Praise Me as though your life depends on it. Because it does."

In that moment, I felt jolted awake. I pressed through and praised God. Within a minute, I felt a breakthrough as despair was obliterated and joy began to stir—not just because of the praise but also because of whom I was praising. It was a practical lesson. Even when it seems like the metaphorical fig trees have no blossoms, we can and must keep rejoicing in the Lord.

LET'S PRAY: "Father, thank You for the gift and weapon of praise. In the middle of troubles, You are the rescue. You are the opportunity in the trouble. I don't have to struggle in the trouble; now the trouble has to bow down to You. In Jesus's name, amen."

But the Lord

The wicked frustrate the plans of the
oppressed, but the Lord will protect his people.
→ Psalm 14:6

There's a war to capture the glorious creativity and boldness of God
within people. People overtaken by evil are held hostage, unable to
release the goodness of God. When we see their behavior, we want
them to get their comeuppance, to learn a lesson. But what we truly
need to do is to see them with the heart of God. Instead of blaming
them, see that they're being held hostage by darkness. Instead of
condemning them, see their actions as an alert to pray for them.

As I was reading today's scripture, I was led to reverse my understanding in the same way and to reread the verse from the heavenly
perspective of Christ. It is true that the wicked frustrate the plans
of the oppressed, but the Lord will protect His people. By the same
token, from a different vantage point, it is also true that *because* the
Lord protects His people, the plans of God will frustrate the plans
of the wicked. Now this stirs my faith in God to a new place. What
about you?

LET'S TALK: How can you see your situation from a different
vantage point? Start looking at it from the perspective of Christ.
What does it look like now? I encourage you to write down this
newfound perspective.

Autocorrect

"My thoughts are nothing like your thoughts," says the Lord. "And my ways are far beyond anything you could imagine. For just as the heavens are higher than the earth, so my ways are higher than your ways and my thoughts higher than your thoughts." → Isaiah 55:8–9

Has your phone ever "corrected" your spelling to something completely incorrect? This happened to me recently. I didn't pay attention until I hit SEND—and realized with horror that by changing one word, my autocorrect feature had changed the entire meaning of my message. I panicked and sent a follow-up text trying to explain the mistake . . . only to realize the same mistake had just happened again! When my friend sent me tons of laughing emojis, I had to just laugh and send an embarrassed emoji in reply. I thought, *How did my phone translate it to that? It wasn't even close!*

It was a hilarious moment, but it also made me realize: This is what I tend to do with God! I try to autocorrect His Word. It's as though I believe God needs my help to make His words make sense. Like when I read that God is for me, I autocorrect it to "God is for me . . . which means He's not for that person who hurt me! I'm God's child, and they have no idea whom they messed with!" Of course, in reality, His Word is clear. He is also for them, and I am to emulate His love by doing what He says: loving my enemies by doing good to those who hurt me, praying for those who persecute me, and blessing those who curse me (Matthew 5:44).

It's never my intent to twist God's words. I'm just speaking from my own thoughts and ways. But today's scripture reveals that His thoughts and ways are much higher than ours, beyond comprehension. I'm learning that whenever I think I can help Him, I really need His help to know He is my Helper.

LET'S TALK: Have you ever autocorrected or mistranslated God's Word? What misconceptions do you have about God? You can give those over to Him right now and ask Him to take them as you experience a divine exchange of your own ideas for His.

Learning Cues

Let everyone see that you are considerate in all you do. Remember, the Lord is coming soon. → Philippians 4:5

We decided to homeschool my daughter for her eighth grade year. Over the first few weeks, it quickly turned from a dream into a hard reality. One day, things escalated so quickly that in a matter of moments, pencils began flying, papers were strewn on the ground, and our shouts of anger grew louder and louder. It was a mess. Suddenly, the "principal" (my husband) burst into the room, and the chaos came to an immediate halt. He had us calmly share our perspectives, one at a time.

As my daughter and I began to talk and share, I realized with a softened heart that I hadn't considered her learning cues. She mastered things by teaching what she was learning. Meanwhile, I wanted to "micro-teach" her in a way that stifled any kind of real learning for her. When we began to see each other's different perspectives, we learned to appreciate each other's strengths and be more mindful of each other's weaknesses. When we show others consideration, as in today's scripture, it comes from the awareness of God's love at every given moment, which is essential to remembering the Lord is coming soon.

LET'S PRAY: "Father God, thank You for Your Holy Spirit, which keeps me aware of Your love that considers others above self. Lord, thank You for helping me value myself so that I properly see others as valuable as well. In Jesus's name, amen."

Just One Touch

With God all things are possible.
→ Matthew 19:26 (ESV)

I helped raise my husband's son, my bonus son (or, as some people say, stepson), from 11 to 19, and although we always loved each other, we sometimes struggled to connect. Soon after he turned 19, he married the love of his life, his high school sweetheart. About seven years later, when we found out he and his wife were having a baby, I was delighted for them, of course, but I was also afraid I wouldn't feel the right kind of connection to my bonus grandson. It led me to pray to God, asking Him to give me the heart connection I so desired.

Although I spent nine months praying with expectation, I never felt any big change within me when thinking about my unborn grandson. But then I laid eyes on him for the first time, right after he was born, as he was lying underneath a warming lamp in the hospital room. As his cries bellowed, I reached out and gently touched his tiny hand. The liquid love of God flowed from the top of my head to the soles of my feet and back. It was a moment I will remember for the rest of my life.

The moment that love rested on me, sweet memories reminded me once again that my grown-up bonus son was simply yet profoundly my son, just as much as if he had been my son his entire life. With just one touch, God used this tiny baby boy to break the levees of my heart with His love.

LET'S TALK: Have you been praying and praying and just feeling nothing? Do you desire for God to break the levees of your heart with His vast love? Give it to Him right now. You may not "feel" anything, but just know by faith that He's working in your heart.

Look Up!

For ever since the world was created, people have seen the earth and sky. Through everything God made, they can clearly see his invisible qualities—his eternal power and divine nature. So they have no excuse for not knowing God. → Romans 1:20

It was one of those difficult seasons in life. There was one particular day when I didn't even want to get out of bed. But I knew I had to get the mail, so I went outside with my head hung low, as I had grown accustomed to looking at the ground. Suddenly, in the depths of my heart, I heard the words "Look up!" It was such a quiet whisper, yet so loud. So I looked up. I was taken aback by the enormous crisp blue sky above me—literally in awe. In that moment, I heard the words, "The sky is as the train of My majestic robe. That is how big I am. Even the heavens cannot contain Me. So why do you try?"

Just thinking about that moment now causes tears to stream down my face. God was rescuing me from hopelessness and opening my ears to hear Him. As I looked up, I saw the vastness of His glory. Even the heavens, without saying a word, proclaim God's glory with such majestic power.

LET'S TALK: Have there been problems in your life that you have allowed to become more magnified than God? Do you want God to be more magnified in your sight? Then look up and open His Word to Psalm 19 today. Step back from the everyday, autopilot movements of life and look at the beauty around you.

Radiant

Those who look to him for help will be radiant with joy; no shadow of shame will darken their faces. → Psalm 34:5

There's no shame in God. So if your face is covered in shame, all you need to realize is that your gaze is on what has been done to you, what you've done to someone else, or even what the enemy has done—rather than what God has done. You need to realize He truly has gone before us. Salvation is accomplished in Him, and we can truly "be radiant with joy," as though we have already received it—because we have.

This is faith. This is what causes the world to look to us in awe as we point others to the Father. When we talk about what the enemy is doing, guess where we've just pointed them? We've pointed them—and ourselves—back to the enemy and his works. That was never our place. We can recognize the works of the enemy, but we must speak the gospel as Jesus did. When we don't know what is ours in Christ, we will constantly be moved, tossed about as if by the waves of the sea (Ephesians 4:14). But when we look to Him, we can't help but be radiant with joy.

LET'S TALK: In what areas of your life can you look to God and joyfully see Him for who He really is? Have you spent more time talking about what the enemy is doing than about who God is? Let this be a reminder to turn your face to God, even in the middle of fear, and stay radiant with joy!

"Righteous" Indignation

What good is it, dear brothers and sisters,
if you say you have faith but don't show it by
your actions? Can that kind of faith
save anyone? → James 2:14

There I was, priding myself on my ability to love those who were hard to love—until I found myself in a situation where I felt attacked. I was full of "righteous" indignation, ranting about what was going on and how absolutely wrong it was. My conversation wasn't solving anything—in fact, it only added fuel to the wildfire. But from my standpoint, it felt so right and just, I didn't pay attention to the fact that it wasn't God's righteousness and justice. I used it as an excuse not to step into God's grace, not to take the opportunity to partner with the Holy Spirit in obedience.

Amazingly enough, while in the middle of a conversation, I heard a divine interruption: "Here's a chance for Me to be seen. Will you reveal Me?" I said to the friend I was talking to, "Oh my goodness! How can God be seen in this and through this?" As I asked, this answer came to me: I could send a card to the person I was mad at, and God would write through me. It would be an encouraging word for her to see Him and His love for her. I could let her know I was praying for her with God's love, and encourage her that He could help her do what is right, if she would just trust Him.

But then I thought, *What if she doesn't get the card? Or what if she laughs at it?* This is when I heard: "Don't worry about that. Your obedience gives Me a way to do the things that only I can do. Just obey. Your obedience is the works behind the faith."

LET'S PRAY: "Father God, thank You for Your outrageous love that instead of becoming indignant declares, 'Father, forgive them for they know not what they do.' Lord, give me Your divine ideas on how to reveal Your love in my situation. I give this to You, Lord. In Jesus's name, amen."

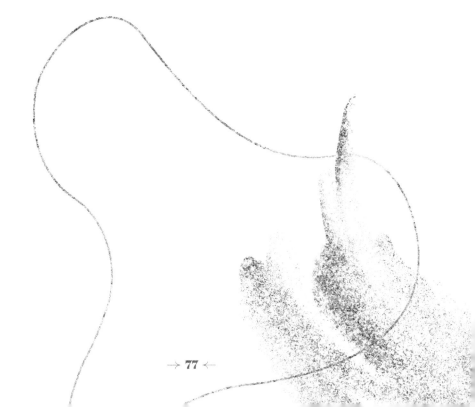

Ending to the Beginning

Put on all of God's armor so that you will be able to stand firm against all strategies of the devil. → Ephesians 6:11

As I opened the Bible app on my phone, I had the desire not just to read but to listen to the book of Ephesians. As I listened, it seemed that everything about living as Christ intended was covered in the six simple yet profound chapters of this letter to the church in Ephesus. Yet even with all the freedom laid out, it still seemed unbelievably daunting. There were so many instructions to follow!

Then it happened: an aha moment in which I was awakened to the Holy Spirit's presence.

This "holy thought" came: When we live in God, we can't help but live out our relationships as He intended. We can't help but be guided by the Holy Spirit as we live in His light. We can't help but live in unity within the body of Christ as Ephesians commands, because we're aware that He is our armor, as today's scripture relates. We can't help but desire not only to pray but also to live a life that reveals spiritual growth. And as we spiritually grow in Him as our armor, we can't help but reveal His mysterious plan, which is Christ in us, the hope of glory!

So, yes, there are guidelines to follow. But if we stop trying to rely on our own self-discipline and just desire to be in Him, we will end up following those guidelines—not with 100 percent perfection, but we'll get there in the long run. Now, doesn't that take some of the pressure off?

LET'S PRAY: "Father God, thank You that I don't have to rely on my own self-discipline to live for You. I am so grateful that with You as my armor, Your discipline comes naturally. Thank You that whenever my old ways begin to flare up, I can flare up in faith. Your faithful promises are my protection. In Jesus's name, amen."

Where's My Phone?

God is our refuge and strength, always ready to help in times of trouble. → Psalm 46:1

My friend and I were on a FaceTime call, laughing hysterically and sharing our hearts as though we were in the same room. In the middle of our conversation, I suddenly realized I didn't know where my phone was. As I continued to talk and listen, I also began to look for my phone in my purse. Next I ran upstairs to check the bathroom counter, then searched my closet. But I couldn't find it anywhere. I finally interrupted our conversation and said, "I can't find my phone!" My friend began laughing and said, "Uh, Teresa, you're on it!" We broke out laughing as I shook my head in disbelief. I was looking for my phone while staring right at it!

Isn't this what we do so often in life with the Holy Spirit? Here we are, going through our everyday moments, the Holy Spirit right there with us. Then something daunting happens and we say, "Lord! Where are You?" All the while, He's right there speaking to us, and often we're not even aware of His gentle voice.

LET'S PRAY: "Father God, thank You for being my refuge and strength, even when I don't notice it. Please help me see You in ways I never imagined. In Jesus's name, amen."

Gummy Vitamins

Try to please them all the time, not just when
they are watching you. As slaves of Christ,
do the will of God with all your heart.
→ Ephesians 6:6

When our daughter was six, we would give her a gummy vitamin
every morning. She would pop it in her mouth, and then we'd leave
for school. This went on for about six months, until one evening,
I felt the redecorating itch. As I slid the bookshelf away from the wall,
something on the floor caught my eye. It was a huge, colorful clump—
six months' worth of gummy vitamins. Apparently, our daughter didn't
want to take her vitamins, and instead of throwing them away, she
decided to hide them under the bookshelf.

As hilarious as this is, it reminds me of those moments when I did
the right thing but my heart wasn't in it—when I was pretending to
take a vitamin even though I was secretly spitting it out. When these
moments arise, let's allow today's scripture to notify our hearts to
shift toward the Lord. No matter what you're doing, you can see it as
an opportunity for an act of worship of Him and Him alone.

TRY THIS TODAY: Write down something you've been doing
even though your heart isn't in it. Now write a prayer of surrender
to the Lord and watch your heart transform until you aren't just
doing that action to please someone else—you're doing it to
please the Lord.

Fishing with the Right Bait

Follow me, and I will show you how to fish for people! → Matthew 4:19

I remember when my husband took our daughter and me fishing with him. Looking at all the different fishing poles and types of bait laid out before us, Tristin and I were a little overwhelmed.

"Why don't you just use the same bait all the time?" I asked.

Selecting the right bait, my husband shared, was part of the sport of fishing. Some types of bait worked better to catch sunfish, whereas others worked better for bass, and yet others for trout. Part of the craft is to know, based on what fish you want to catch, where to fish, when to fish, and what strategy to use, including what kind of bait to put on your line.

I never viewed fishing the same way again. And I better understood why Jesus said He'd make the disciples "fishers of men." Jesus knows that every person is different, and although there's only one gospel, it can reach people in different ways. The same goes for parenting, too; whether we have one child or more, we learn that kids are all unique. We must approach them all differently in order to raise them effectively, with the help of the Holy Spirit, who is the master fisherman.

TRY THIS TODAY: As you assess your children, don't do it on your own understanding. First, go to God and ask Him how He sees them. From there, think about their personality traits—strengths, weaknesses, and quirks—and begin to see how each trait can be used for God's glory. Write those traits down and pray about them. You can even pray Matthew 4:19 over your children right now, whether they're in front of you at the moment or not.

Walking Aware

They said to each other, "Didn't our hearts
burn within us as he talked with us on the road
and explained the Scriptures to us?"
→ Luke 24:32

My daughter and I were walking together, talking and enjoying the wind blowing in our hair. As we walked, we discussed how we wanted to be intentionally aware of the presence of God in that moment. As we spoke, I looked over at my daughter and said, "Tristin, I don't want to look back through my life and finally realize that Jesus was there the entire time. I want to be aware of Him in the now."

That was the moment that brought me to the story revealed in Luke 24. I tried to imagine that scene as the two disciples were on the road to Emmaus. Here they were, walking along and running into a man they didn't recognize. As he talked with them, they had no idea it was Jesus, and they only realized later that it had been Him all along. That seems to be a natural tendency, doesn't it? There are moments when we don't look for Him because we feel we have the answer—when all along, the answer Himself is waiting on us to invite Him into our every situation.

LET'S TALK: How much richer would those great moments be if we invited the Lord into our life, which He allows us to live? It's like a dance of sorts. He invited us into this life by creating us, and we get to invite Him back.

Focus

And let us run with endurance the
race God has set before us. We do this by
keeping our eyes on Jesus, the champion who
initiates and perfects our faith. Because of
the joy awaiting him, he endured the cross,
disregarding its shame. Now he is seated in
the place of honor beside God's throne.
→ Hebrews 12:1–2

It was an early spring evening, years ago. My daughter, Tristin, and I were walking to the playground when we decided to play a silly game. The goal was to stay focused despite our own individual distractions. My daughter's weakness was cats; mine was smelling the flowers along the way. I said to Tristin, "As we walk down the sidewalk, no matter how many cats come our way or how many flowers we see, let's stay focused and keep walking until we get to the playground."

Tristin giggled at this proposition, and on we went, trying to follow our new rule. We quickly realized it wouldn't be as easy as it sounded. As soon as we decided to play this seemingly silly game, it seemed like more flowers were blooming than ever before and more cats than we'd ever seen met us along the way.

This moment reminded me of just how easy it is to be seduced away from God by what's going on in this life. It's no wonder Jesus was emphatic about us staying in Him. The only way to stay focused is to keep our eyes fixed on Him, the champion of our faith, allowing Him to be our divine intention in the midst of every other diversion.

LET'S PRAY: "Father God, in the name of Jesus, thank You for Your goodness that helps us when the world is trying to seduce us away from You. Thank You for being the Way for us to follow. In Jesus's name, amen."

Don't Give Up, Give In!

So let's not get tired of doing what is good. At just the right time we will reap a harvest of blessing if we don't give up. → Galatians 6:9

Sweat. Tears of frustration. The temptation to give up. Thoughts of the unknown plagued all of our minds when our son, Cody, took up wrestling from middle school into high school. Would he work hard? Would he get hurt? Would his mind be strong even when things didn't go his way? There were so many moments when my husband placed his arm around Cody as tears of discouragement rolled down our son's face.

During one particular match, the crowd roared as Cody stepped out onto the mat. Our emotions stirred as we heard the echoing voices shouting, "Cody! Go, Cody! Come on, Cody!" The sound of feet stomping on bleachers permeated the gymnasium. Cody and his opponent met in the middle of the mat and shook hands. The referee blew the whistle, and the match began. Our son had been fighting frustration, the temptation to give up, and a lack of confidence. He really wasn't sure he could do this. But by the end, the crowd stood up and cheered as Cody, undefeated, placed another victory under his belt.

Tears welled up in my eyes as I saw Cody shake his opponent's hand and walk off the mat, headed toward his biggest fan and life coach: his dad. It was the moment that all those other small moments were all about. But the most rewarding part was seeing Cody encouraging all his wrestling teammates that night, just as his dad had encouraged him. The encouraged son became the encourager, the coached became the coach, and the embraced was now embracing others.

LET'S TALK: Are we reflecting our Father God? Ask yourself: I have been encouraged by God—am I now encouraging others? I have been taught by God—am I going to start teaching others what I have learned, not only with what I say but also with what I do? I have been lavishly and lovingly embraced by God—am I now embracing others, no matter what or where they are in their lives?

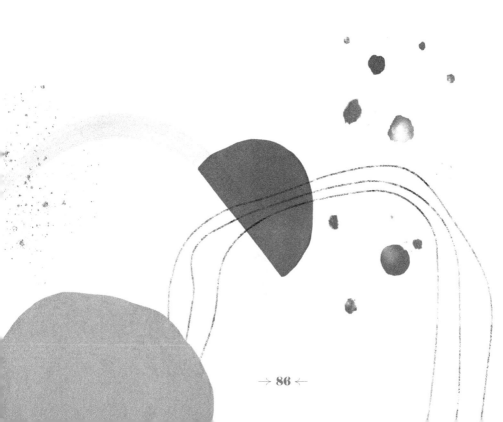

Trust, Rest, Live

Those who live in the shelter of the Most High
will find rest in the shadow of the Almighty.
This I declare about the Lord: He alone is my
refuge, my place of safety; he is my God,
and I trust him. → Psalm 91:1–2

In today's scripture, I noticed these words: Live. Rest. Trust. When you *trust* God, you can *rest*, and in that rest, you can truly *live*. What an honor that God would allow us to live in Him, resting in His shadow. I believe I can safely assume that Moses, the author of this particular psalm, undoubtedly knew God as his safe place. Moses knew Him as refuge and even safety.

I wonder whether this is how our children feel with us on an earthly level. Have you ever noticed how when they're smaller, they see us as their everything? It's as though there's nothing we can't do in their eyes. Sometimes we think, "If they only knew how flawed I am!" Although we can't guarantee perfection to our children, our God guarantees it to us. What a promise! May you trust, rest, and live in Him today.

LET'S PRAY: "Father God, thank You for being my safety, refuge, and shield. As I am learning to live in You, it's because I can trust that I can rest in You. Father, I thank You for being closer than close. In Jesus's name, amen."

Honored Awe

And behold, a woman in the city who was a sinner, when she knew that Jesus sat at the table in the Pharisee's house, brought an alabaster flask of fragrant oil, and stood at His feet behind Him weeping; and she began to wash His feet with her tears, and wiped them with the hair of her head; and she kissed His feet and anointed them with the fragrant oil. → Luke 7:37–38 (NKJV)

I so much want to witness every moment that she wept over him, kissing His feet. She is the woman we still read and talk about until this very day, some 2,000 years later. This woman desperately entered this Pharisee's house, an intruder from the viewpoint of many onlookers. The overwhelming love of Jesus overtook her as she wept, broke the beautiful alabaster box, and poured the expensive fragrant oil upon his feet.

What does that moment represent to me? What is so dear to me, like that valuable box and its expensive contents, that I dare not part with it? Would I be able to break free and give it to Jesus?

I imagine the strands of her hair, the glory of her head, getting to touch the feet of Jesus. As the people around Him acted insulted by such a display, Jesus saw her with overwhelming compassion and amazing, unfailing love. Overtaken by this woman's honor for Him, He spoke forgiveness of the sins she had committed, releasing her with great blessing as He told her to go in peace. I am in awe. It draws me to desire that intimate moment with Him, one that can never be compared to intimacy with anything or anyone else.

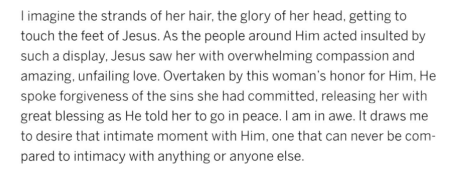

LET'S TALK: Are you in awe of this woman's life? Do you desire to be in awe of God for the rest of your days? We can start by being in awe of God's great love. Don't let yourself grow numb to it. Do you want to lavishly love Him like she did? Be bold today, knowing that He loves you and He wants you to love Him so that you can begin loving yourself as He intended. Today be led and drawn to His magnificent presence, weeping uncontrollably, just as this woman did when she beheld Him with great honor.

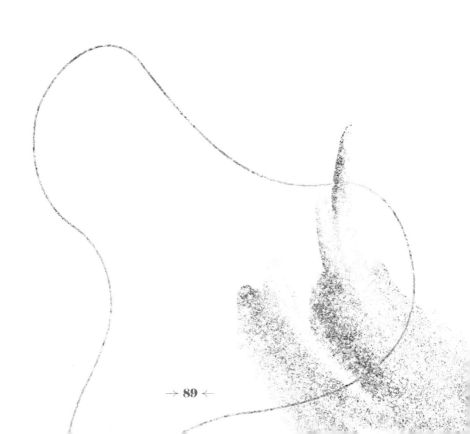

Waking Up

And being found in appearance as a man, He humbled Himself and became obedient to the point of death, even the death of the cross. Therefore God also has highly exalted Him and given Him the name which is above every name, that at the name of Jesus every knee should bow, of those in heaven, and of those on earth, and of those under the earth, and that every tongue should confess that Jesus Christ is Lord, to the glory of God the Father.
→ Philippians 2:8–11 (NKJV)

Once, when my daughter was young, I said, "Tristin, you know what boggles my mind? God doesn't sleep."

"I know," she said. "He watches over us while we sleep."

"But Tristin, you know how sometimes God will wake us up in the middle of the night because He wants to talk?"

"Yes."

"Well, you know how groggy you are when we try waking you up? Can you imagine if I woke you up in the middle of the night just to talk?" We laughed as we imitated our sleepy selves dreading the thought of waking up. I continued, "God is not limited to time. He is eternal."

"He's nocturnal?" my daughter asked.

I laughed. "No, honey, He's *eternal*. What we think of as interrupted sleep, He may think of as just another moment. I can imagine Him saying, 'Teresa, wake up! I want to tell you something. Wake up!' And when I'm finally awake, I can hear Him say, 'I just wanted to say I love you. That's all.'"

Think about this. Jesus, the Word of God, was made flesh. He gave up all His divinity, His limitless eternity, and took the form of a human being who gets tired, falls asleep, and wakes up groggy. Jesus may have been poor on Earth, but the riches of the world are nothing compared to the heavenly riches He gave up to save us.

LET'S PRAY: "Father God, I am amazed that You never grow weary. It is incredible, Jesus, that You would give up your right to be God to do the will of the Father so that I could live in Your freedom. Today, help me be aware of Your presence. In Jesus's name, amen."

Awe-Inspired

Then God looked over all he had made, and he saw that it was very good! And evening passed and morning came, marking the sixth day.
→ Genesis 1:31

It was a gorgeous day, so I decided to bring my canvas and paints outside to be creative in the backyard with only the sky as a ceiling. I began to worship God as I painted, playing praise songs on my phone. It didn't matter to me what my artwork looked like, because I was so aware of the glimpses of His splendid presence. I didn't want the moments to end. There was a closeness and an intimacy with the Father that caused every mind-confining box to disintegrate.

An awareness of God's creativity flowed through me as I painted. I knew this awareness came from the Lord as it led me back to the beginning, to Genesis. After everything God created, He looked at it and said, "It is good." With that reminder, the sweet whisper of the Holy Spirit shared with me, "Every time you finish a painting, illustration, or piece of writing, I want you to look at it and declare, 'It is good!'" This is another expression of how to love God with our everything, so we can love ourselves and in turn love others as ourselves. Once we see the value of God in us, we can then value others as God intended.

LET'S TALK: What creative thing, big or small, have you done as worship of the Lord? Take a moment to think of that creative work, or even a chore or work assignment. Then lift it up to the Lord and say, "Thank You, Father, it is good."

Faith and Hope

Faith shows the reality of what we hope for;
it is the evidence of things we cannot see.
→ Hebrews 11:1

When a woman is pregnant, she can use an ultrasound to see the sweet baby in her womb. The image may be grainy, and from the outside she may not even look pregnant yet. But hidden within her, a new life is forming. Faith is like that ultrasound image. You may see it only faintly, but once you get a glimpse of it, you enter a whole new dimension of reality. No one else can see it, but the glimpse you received is evidence of another realm that's about to collide with yours. And no matter how much time passes, you can't unsee it.

So it is with the desires that God has placed within us. Yet the reality of what we hope for is not just in something earthly or monetary that we have desired. It's so much more than that! It's seeing the evidence of God, in which faith and hope work together in such a powerful way. A sign that points us to God Himself, to desire and hope in Him and Him alone!

LET'S PRAY: "Father God, sharpen my awareness to see with eyes of faith while hoping in You and You alone. Thank You, Lord, that in the midst of distractions, I will be divinely distracted by Your goodness, which gives tangible evidence of who You are! In Jesus's name, amen."

A Lesson from the Ants

Take a lesson from the ants, you lazybones.
Learn from their ways and become wise!
Though they have no prince or governor or
ruler to make them work, they labor hard all
summer, gathering food for the winter.
→ Proverbs 6:6–8

Lying out in our backyard, I flipped over on my stomach to get some sun on my back and saw a tiny ant crawling on a blade of grass. I began to consider the value of insects and suddenly noticed a whole new world I hadn't paid attention to before. Normally I would scream at just the sight of a bug, but in that moment, I became a student of creation, in magnificent awe of the Creator.

It was as though God was enlarging my heart for things I usually saw as insignificant. It was a moment, as it says in today's scripture, to learn from their ways. Think about how essential they are to our ecosystem. They're like little clean-up crews, and the nests they build even help aerate the soil. God made me take notice of these details of His loving nature. It made me want more of Him. I was lying face-down, but He lifted my eyes up to see things the way He sees them, illuminating my heart to want Him even more.

LET'S PRAY: "Lord, enlarge my heart for Your creation, so that I can start to see it how You see it. I want to live in You without outside motivation; I just want it to be an innate response to You. In Jesus's name, amen."

Heart Transplant

Take delight in the Lord, and he will give you your heart's desires. → Psalm 37:4

"Okay, Lord, I will delight in You . . . *if* You give me my heart's desires." Doesn't that sound laughable? Yet my laugh is hesitant, because I've had this thought quite often. It sort of seemed to work at first, until I realized that whenever I drew close to Him with my own agenda, the items on that agenda would fall away. As I delighted in Him, my human desires were transformed into divine desires that I had never dreamed or imagined.

For most of my life, I saw Psalm 37:4 as an "if/then" statement. *If* you take delight in the Lord, *then* you'll get the things you want. Little did I know that pure delight in God would change all the things I wanted, or that this would make me feel joy beyond my understanding. I believe He gives us the desires He has dreamed for us, placing them within us like a divine heart transplant. And what we desire most of all is Him. God is our dream come true.

LET'S TALK: What have you desired more than God Himself? Whatever it is, will you surrender it? The way to surrender is to constantly delight in the Lord. The delight *is* the surrender. There's no effort required on your part; praising Him causes an automatic change of heart, in which your desires are replaced with His!

You Have Everything You Need

Now you have every spiritual gift you need as you eagerly wait for the return of our Lord Jesus Christ. He will keep you strong to the end so that you will be free from all blame on the day when our Lord Jesus Christ returns. God will do this, for he is faithful to do what he says, and he has invited you into partnership with his Son, Jesus Christ our Lord.
→ 1 Corinthians 1:7–9

It is mind-blowing to realize we don't need to look around or worry—we already have every spiritual gift we'll ever need. That's because the Holy Spirit lives within us. Think about it this way: Every need, concern, or problem we have, He's the solution. He doesn't just provide a way; He *is* the Way. That alone is incredible.

And according to today's scripture, we have been given these spiritual gifts for a very important purpose: so that we are able to eagerly wait for the return of our Lord Jesus Christ. The Holy Spirit keeps us strong even during the moments when we want to default to our natural weaknesses. It lifts us up when we would otherwise crumble. It gives us the ability to remain steady.

It's amazing how the Holy Spirit gives us this miraculous strength so that we'll be free from all blame on the day when Jesus returns. God is faithful to do what He has said, and He has invited each of us into a relationship with Jesus. Now that's evidence that we have everything we need in life. After all, He is our everything.

LET'S TALK: Do you see how the Holy Spirit of God wants to refresh you with who He is? He is so full of faith in you to trust Him as your everything. When you have a moment, write a letter to God (perhaps in your journal) and watch Him begin to write to you and through you.

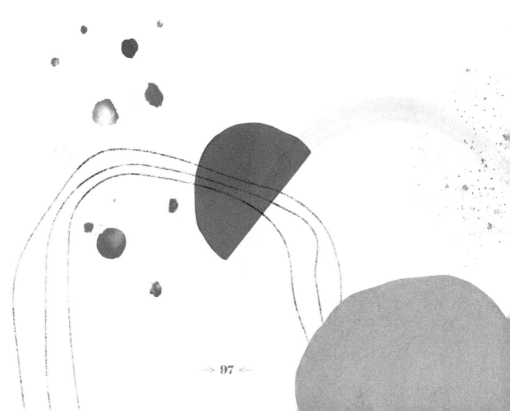

Mama Duck

Direct your children onto the right path, and
when they are older, they will not leave it.
→ Proverbs 22:6

Today's scripture reminds me of the time my family and I watched a
mother duck waddling down the road as her baby ducklings formed a
line behind her. We admired the maternal instinct of this mama duck,
guiding her babies as they watched her lead by example. They followed where she went, and she directed them in the right way to go.

So it is with leaders and parents. There are those looking up to and
watching us as they follow. How are we directing our children? Are
we directing them in the way we want them to go? Or in the way God
wants? If we want them to follow us, then let's follow after the Lord
as He leads and guides us with His love that powerfully demonstrates
who He is. As we follow Him like baby ducklings, our children will be
led to follow Him as well.

TRY THIS TODAY: Write down three areas in which you want to
lead your children better. Then go to the Lord and share what you
wrote with Him. As you share, pay attention to how He's guiding you.

Childlike

On a good day, enjoy yourself; on a bad day, examine your conscience. God arranges for both kinds of days so that we won't take anything for granted. → Ecclesiastes 7:14 (MSG)

I was walking through the store in a huge hurry, because, well, I was used to being in a hurry. There were grocery lists to keep on top of and schedules to stick to. As I approached the checkout line, I turned around to find that my daughter wasn't right behind me as I'd assumed. To my surprise, she had lagged behind me to play with a Hula-Hoop.

Now normally, in moments like this, I would have had a fit. Why wasn't she paying attention? She could have been kidnapped! Why didn't she stick by my side in the store like she'd been taught? My default was to feel worried, irritated, upset—anything but happy. But in this moment, I was fully aware of a teaching lesson from the Holy Spirit: "Your daughter is teaching you how to live. Now pay attention. Come to Me as a child—not childish, but childlike." My impulse had been to teach her by scolding her, but now I saw that she was going to teach me.

In that moment, I entered her world—a child's world of just enjoying life. Her enjoyment was a sweet demonstration of gratitude for being alive. I grabbed my own Hula-Hoop and began to try to make it spin. Although we failed to get them to twirl around us, what was left swirling was sweet laughter and a beautiful memory of the day.

LET'S PRAY: "Father God, thank You for the Holy Spirit that lets me consider this life as a gift from You. Lord, thank You for the awareness that this life is but a vapor, and to enjoy these moments. And when the days are hard, help me go to You as You examine my heart. In Jesus's name, amen."

You Are Forgiven

Then Jesus said to the woman,
"Your sins are forgiven." → Luke 7:48

Years ago, when my daughter, Tristin, was 12, we had a serious talk. I told her about some sins in my past, and then I asked her for forgiveness. To my surprise, she began to cry and said, "No! I can't forgive you. My mom would never do that." In that moment, I felt deep regret for bringing the subject up with her. Maybe she wasn't yet the right age to have these kinds of talks.

But then I received this thought: "She believes that if she forgives you, she would be saying that what you did was okay. She needs to know that forgiveness validates the person, not the sin." I realized I was being taught what forgiveness looked like, right as I was being led to teach my daughter the same thing.

As my daughter cried, I tried to hug her, but she pulled away. I said, "Tristin, do you believe that if you forgive Mommy, you'd be saying what I did was okay?"

"Yes," she sobbed.

With relief, I understood I'd heard the Spirit of God. I simply said, "Tristin, when you forgive Mommy, you're not saying that what I did was okay. You're just saying that I'm okay with God now."

Suddenly she stopped crying. She looked at me with a huge smile and said, "I forgive you, Mom!" As she walked away, I felt I had just experienced a moment with Jesus, like the woman in today's scripture. Can you imagine hearing the words "Your sins are forgiven"? I felt a snap as I was released from shame into the freedom Jesus has given us, as He is our Freedom.

LET'S TALK: Are there people you haven't forgiven? Is it because you feel that if you did, you would be saying what they did was okay? Today, let's walk this out together. As God validates us and not our sin, let's do the same for others.

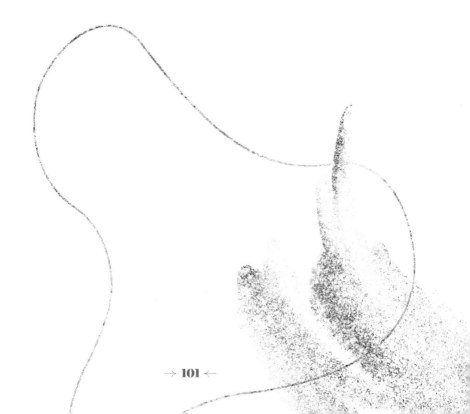

There's a Choice to Be Made

Today I have given you the choice between life and death, between blessings and curses. Now I call on heaven and earth to witness the choice you make. Oh, that you would choose life, so that you and your descendants might live! → Deuteronomy 30:19

When I'm in a place of unbelief, fear, and doubt, it reveals my lack of trust and reliance on God. When I feel like I no longer have control of my life, I panic—only to realize that I have yet again failed myself by trying to be self-reliant instead of God-reliant.

But that doesn't mean I can use the excuse "Well, God is in control" to avoid making choices. Yes, He is in control . . . but He gave us free will so that we can choose life instead of death. So that we can choose to see through the lens of His great love instead of our own clouded lenses. It saddens my heart to know that I have used His gift of free will to reject the things of Him, due to my slanted perception of reality. But I am always happy when I manage to see the world through His eyes and make the right choices because of it.

TRY THIS TODAY: Wouldn't it be great to become a rebel for the cause of Jesus? Rebel against yourself when you don't want to choose Him. See this as something you *get* to do instead of something you have to do.

Pray, Forgive, Pray

I tell you, you can pray for anything, and if you
believe that you've received it, it will be yours.
But when you are praying, first forgive anyone
you are holding a grudge against, so that your
Father in heaven will forgive your sins, too.
→ Mark 11:24–25

I couldn't stop thinking about my outrage over the way a friend had
spoken to me. Many years after it happened, I was still replaying that
hurtful moment like a broken record. The more I nurtured the pain,
the more my demeanor revealed hurt and anger as I unknowingly fed
the appetite of bitterness.

Even though I was surrounded by the beauty of God revealed through
my loving family, I didn't pay attention to it. I was too intent on giving
a place to the hurt, consumed with how I felt I had been wronged.
Maybe I had a "right" to be angry about how my friend had treated
me, but that anger infringed on my rightful promise to be walking in
the joy of the Lord. I had allowed it to trespass and keep me from the
blessings of life.

I believe this is one of the many reasons why Jesus said to forgive
others before praying in today's scripture. He knows that when we
stand in unforgiveness, we can try to pray, but we're communicating
through our wronged perception rather than His heavenly perspective. Prayer should echo back what the Word of God says over a
person or situation, not what has already happened. We don't need
to keep meditating on our pain and hurt. We need to let go of it as we
increase our awareness of Him.

LET'S PRAY: "Lord God, any grip that is on my life that is not of You I repent and renounce. As I have received Your blessing so freely, I now freely bless all those who have hurt me. Lord, remind me that forgiveness does not validate wrongdoing; it only validates that You want everyone to know Your love as I do. Father, at every trigger, let me be triggered to run to You. I thank You for Your gift of forgiveness. In Jesus's name, amen."

Applauding Him with Our Lives

Come, everyone! Clap your hands! Shout to God with joyful praise! For the Lord Most High is awesome. He is the great King of all the earth. → Psalm 47:1–2

It wasn't his great ability, stature, or strength that allowed David to kill Goliath—it was his ferocious faith in God. He had so much confidence in the One he served and worshiped, the giant didn't have a chance. Likewise, it is not our abilities, knowledge, or experiences that will make us overcomers. Rather, it's a relationship with the One who overcame it all for us—the one and only God, who is revealed through our lives as we have accepted Him as our Savior.

I don't want to be led by *a* spirit. I want to be led by *the* Holy Spirit of God. Think of the great feats we can accomplish with this life in Christ! There is no limit. We get to applaud the Lord with our very lives, moment by moment. I want it to be like a heartbeat in my life, so that I can't help but applaud Him just by living.

LET'S PRAY: "Father God, I want to applaud You with my life, and I know that can happen when I remain in You, because You are love. Lord, I want to trust that no matter what is going on around me, You are the Author and the Finisher of my faith. In Jesus's name, amen."

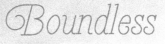

Boundless

But will God really live on earth?
Why, even the highest heavens cannot contain
you. How much less this Temple I have built!
→ 1 Kings 8:27

We live lives defined by boundaries. We are conceived within the boundaries of the womb, and we live within the boundaries of a home. We have social boundaries that govern things like how close we stand to others in public. These boundaries are invisible, but we know them well and live by them.

There is safety within boundaries. But they can also limit us, especially if we start trying to contain God within them. We might find it difficult to imagine doing certain things that God has placed within us, because we've unknowingly told ourselves they're beyond us. We generally look at "crossing the line" as a defiant act of disobedience, but it can also be an awesome act of obedience to God. When people say, "There's no way, that's impossible," God says, "There is a way, for I have made a way." Even though I live in a world that is filled with boundaries, I want to be totally dependent on God, who has no boundaries, for even the heavens cannot contain His amazing glory!

LET'S PRAY: "Father God, I praise You because You are boundless. With great faith in You, I want to see what seemingly impossible things You do in my life. As the heavens declare Your glory, they are unable to contain You. In Jesus's name, amen."

Grace That Brags on God

God saved you by his grace when you believed. And you can't take credit for this; it is a gift from God. Salvation is not a reward for the good things we have done, so none of us can boast about it. → Ephesians 2:8–9

As I once heard worship musician Rick Pino say, "God doesn't just want a relationship with us; He desires fellowship with us." It made me realize that God desires a deep relationship—a divine entanglement of sorts.

This reminds me of some insightful and profound conversations I had just this past week. The common thread in so many of them was the goodness of God and His faithfulness. So many of these conversations focused on proclaiming His empowering grace, which is sufficient—in fact, more than enough—for us to sustain the blows of this life with the wherewithal to keep standing. Without that grace, our circumstances could easily destroy us. With it, we're invincible.

Through the difficult challenges and rigorous testing of life, when we choose God's grace, something new is born. And just like when giving birth, the pain can be excruciating, but the memory of the pain is replaced with joy in the midst of the grueling labor of that season of life.

Let's think about what grace does. It saves us, of course, but it also "brags on" God—it shows everyone in the world how great He is. It gives glory to Him as it reveals Him as the Sustainer and the One who carries us—our armor and our protection. Grace reveals that He is the living breath that causes us to endure, the wind that allows us to soar above devastation. Those moments we messed up, the mistakes we made, the efforts that seemed to be wasted . . . His grace fills in the gaps. He is the bridge to help us cross over to the other side of a great divide.

TRY THIS TODAY: When you look back, even in just the last season, how has grace bragged on God in your life? Write your findings down in your journal.

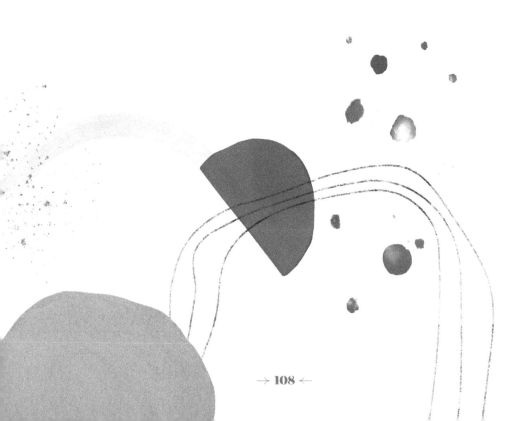

Catch-Up

And we are confident that he hears us whenever we ask for anything that pleases him. And since we know he hears us when we make our requests, we also know that he will give us what we ask for. → 1 John 5:14–15

Many times when I've prayed, especially as a mom, it's seemed to be from a place of fear: a fear of loss, a fear of life not going the way I'd planned. But in moments when I've caught myself praying out of fear, I've realized I wasn't praying at all. I've learned that if I really understood whom I was going to in prayer, I would feel awe and wonder. If I were coming from a truly prayerful posture, I would know whom I'm speaking to and who is speaking back to me.

When we look at our own lives, it's easy to get caught up in the details and the unknowns. We can see minor tiffs as all-consuming battles and, conversely, see prayer or worship as something non-urgent that we can get around to later. But God is not playing catch-up with us. Quite the contrary—we're catching up to His unfolding story of grace. So when we pray, let's pray according to the knowledge that He is who He says He is, and He will give us what we need.

LET'S TALK: Have you ever prayed in fear? What steps can you take to make sure that in the future, you pray from a place of knowing that God gives us what we need?

Crying Out for Someone Else

I am the good shepherd; I know my own sheep, and they know me, just as my Father knows me and I know the Father. So I sacrifice my life for the sheep. → John 10:14-15

Have you heard of Desmond Doss? He was the pacifist combat medic who inspired the movie *Hacksaw Ridge*. He never carried a weapon while he saved soldiers on the battlefield; instead, he prayed, "Please, Lord, help me get one more." With that prayer, by the power of God, he saved over 70 men on what some consider the bloodiest battlefield of World War II—all without firing a shot. No matter how often he was mocked, threatened, and beaten for his faith, he remained true to his selfless mission.

What if we did the same? Of course, most of us won't be saving soldiers on the battlefield, but have we stopped to consider that our lives aren't about what *we* "need," but rather about others and the One, and what *they* need? Whenever you have a thought like "Look at all I've done for this person," let that be your reminder that the self needs to surrender yet again to God's love. His love doesn't keep records of wrongs, which means He doesn't want us to keep records of what we have done right either. This is our worship of Him.

TRY THIS TODAY: Whenever you find yourself asking a question that focuses on the self, try shifting your perspective and reversing it. Instead of "Why has no one comforted me?" ask, "Whom can I comfort?" Instead of "Why is everyone surrounded by friends but me?" ask, "Whom can I surround with friendship?"

Who's Listening?

Let your conversation be gracious and attractive so that you will have the right response for everyone. → Colossians 4:6

A friend of mine—who doesn't go to church but had been *so* close to visiting—overheard two women talking loudly as they had breakfast together at a local restaurant. Their conversation was plagued with gossip, venting, and speaking poorly about their "friends" and leaders within their church. As this friend told me what they'd overheard, they said, "I wanted to go over to their table and let them know they just confirmed why I don't go to church. But then the Holy Spirit convicted me, as I would be pointing out a splinter in their eye when I have a plank in my own, because I've done the same thing."

I was impressed by my friend's maturity, but in the same moment, my heart dropped. I thought, *God bless those ladies, they have no idea what they just did.* Oblivious to who was around, they'd helped prevent my friend (and who knows how many other people) from going to church. It was a reminder to me to follow today's scripture and hope that I wouldn't do the same.

LET'S TALK: If others were to overhear your conversations, would it bring grace to them? If not, repent to the Lord for those moments you haven't pleased Him with your talk. Ask God to minister to anyone who has heard negative and foul talk come from your own mouth.

100 Years from Now

You can make many plans, but the Lord's purpose will prevail. → Proverbs 19:21

A friend of mine recently posted the following question on their blog: "Will this trivial thing that I am upset about matter in 100 years?" It's a great reminder to notice where our awareness is focused. Are our eyes on people and temporary things? Or are they on the eternal goodness of God? His truth trumps our "facts," whatever we think they are in the moment. His hope and grace, rather than our day-to-day worries, must be declared as the final word.

If I am here to leave a legacy, whose legacy is it I want to leave behind? My own? Someone else's? Or the One who has the greatest legacy of all, Jesus Christ? Just asking those questions can cause a great adjustment within our hearts, letting Him transform them as we work out our salvation daily. It's a reminder that even though this life is but a vapor, we can seize every second as an intentional moment of worship of the King of Kings.

LET'S PRAY: "Father God, thank You for the reminder of the brevity of life so that I stay aware of Your presence within me by Your Holy Spirit. It's in my weakness that I can surrender my everything, which is so minute in comparison to You, and yet Your strength is seen in the midst of it all. In Jesus's name, amen."

Fear of the Lord

Fear of the Lord teaches wisdom; humility precedes honor. → Proverbs 15:33

There I was, a mom of two who had just started working, and I really wanted to be a great employee. My focus was on impressing the management team and being a "breath of fresh air" to others.

Yet the more I focused on how people saw me, the closer I got to fearing people rather than God. And the closer I got to that, the more exhausted and miserable I became.

But these were teaching moments with the Lord. He allowed me to think about my children. Would I want them to strive for earthly approval like this all the days of their lives? No way! That's when I realized that God doesn't want that for us, either. Fear of people doesn't reveal anything but pride, whereas fear of the Lord reveals honor, causing humility to make God's mark, revealing His divine power.

So I knew it was a moment to listen. God took my striving and highlighted how it was rooted in pride, how I had listened to lying fears. He showed me that He didn't create any of us to make an impression but rather to make an impact for His glory. And the only way this could happen would be to focus on the Lord. When our awareness is on God's heart rather than career advancement, that's when we make an impact for God's glory.

TRY THIS TODAY: Throughout your day, begin noticing why you're doing what you're doing. If you did something well but you notice you did it for your own ego, turn the motive around and do it as an act of worship. Just watch: You might be doing the same action, but now you'll be doing it with joy that ministers to the people around you. And even if no one shows appreciation, you get to remind yourself that it was for the Lord.

Find the Gold

If you search for good, you will find favor;
but if you search for evil, it will find you!
→ Proverbs 11:27

When our son was in high school, he did very well, and it was rare for us to have any issues with each other. However, there was one thing that was a constant thorn in my side: He was chewing tobacco. And the more I confronted him about it, the more he denied it.

One day, I set out to prove to him that the Holy Spirit would always eventually reveal any secret he tried to conceal. Clearly, I had yet to learn that it's never good to use the Holy Spirit as a means to condemn or prove a point.

So, for an entire week, I went looking for the thing I suspected my son of doing. And like clockwork, guess what happened? I would find what I was looking for and eagerly rub it in his face to prove my point.

One day, I was on the search yet again, adrenaline rushing as I sought out what I was bound and determined to locate. But then a divine moment of interruption took place. I'll never forget how I saw these words, almost as clearly as if they were being projected onto a screen: "If you put as much energy into finding what's *right* about your son as you have into finding what's *wrong*, this whole situation would be different. Don't be surprised that the more you search for dirt, the more you find it. Now, pray that you find the gold in him, and seek Me so you can see what I see and say about him."

Soon after, I was led to today's scripture, which I share with you.

LET'S TALK: What have you been searching for? Are you intentionally looking to find out where God is in your situation? Or are you expecting calamity and negativity? Today, surrender your expectations and begin looking for the goodness of God in your moments.

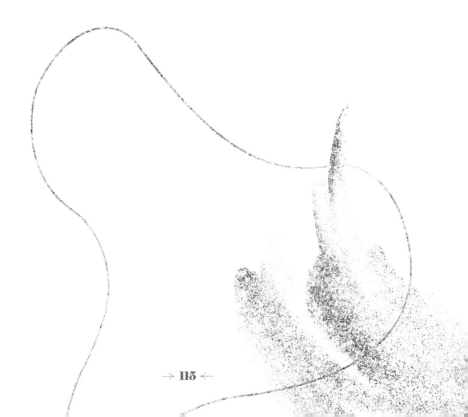

I Just Want to Walk Again

Open for me the gates where the righteous enter, and I will go in and thank the Lord. These gates lead to the presence of the Lord, and the godly enter there. I thank you for answering my prayer and giving me victory! → Psalm 118:19–21

In the waiting room at the doctor's office, I spotted a woman in a wheelchair checking in for her appointment. As she waited, she began crying softly to herself. I'm sure it was a moment she thought no one would see—which was most likely why the Holy Spirit moved me with the words "Be My embrace." After I'd introduced myself, I felt a nudge to ask, "What can I pray about with you?" Her answer has not left me. As tears streamed down her face, she whispered, "I just want to walk again."

We grabbed each other's hands and prayed that she would walk again. I believe she will, and if she doesn't here on earth, she will one day in eternity. God has a purpose for her, no matter what. God doesn't value or love us based on our abilities or disabilities. He loves His children, and He hears our cries for help as well as our prayers of gratitude.

LET'S PRAY: "Father God, let me see more clearly again with Your love. Help me share Your love with others, and help others share Your love with me. In Jesus's name, amen."

Growing Endurance

Dear brothers and sisters, when troubles of any kind come your way, consider it an opportunity for great joy. For you know that when your faith is tested, your endurance has a chance to grow. → James 1:2–3

When my family and I garden, we do as much as we can to ensure that the seeds have a chance to grow. We steward them daily, watering and caring for them, making sure they stay nestled deep in the nutritious soil. And then, sure enough, after we wait a little while, we begin to see little green shoots of life coming through the dirt.

But when I think about it, I also think of the struggle and discomfort of the seed within the dirt—the splitting open that has to take place within the darkness of the soil in order for the plant to finally grow toward the sun.

That's what today's scripture reminds me of. A seed is not defined by any single part of the process, but when you put together all the moments of struggle and darkness, they let the seed reach its full potential as a beautiful plant.

Without discomfort, there can be no growth. And without growth, we can't become who God wants us to be. That's why James says that "troubles of any kind" are actually "opportunities for great joy": They give us the chance to grow.

LET'S TALK: As with seeds, there are no loopholes or shortcuts that let us skip the process of growth. Notice that James didn't write, "Consider it an opportunity for great joy, unless it's that thing that's really hard for you." What is the loophole you need to give to God? Write it down, then write or say, "God! Although this issue doesn't bring me joy, You are my joy, and You bring me supernatural strength to deal with it. I am thankful for this opportunity to grow in the knowledge of who You are. In Jesus's name, amen."

Do I Know You?

And you yourself must be an example to
them by doing good works of every kind.
Let everything you do reflect the integrity and
seriousness of your teaching. → Titus 2:7

In Texas, you can do many of your daily errands in drive-throughs:
deposit or withdraw money at the bank, pay your bills, and so on.
As I tried to enter one such drive-through to pay my utilities bill,
I miscalculated the turn. Suddenly, my daughter and I were jolted
up out of our seats as my truck bounced off the median. We were
uninjured, but my pride took a hit when I saw a few of the employees watching us through the glass window. They were covering their
mouths in shock. Not knowing what else to do, I burst into nervous
laughter and waved at them.

When I rolled down the window to pay my bill, I heard the woman who
was working start giggling over the intercom. "Did you think you were
driving a monster truck?" she asked.

"Oh, you know I did that on purpose, right?" I joked.

Still laughing nervously, I apologized for the commotion as I sent
my credit card through the drive-through's pneumatic tube. A few
moments later, the intercom came back on. I heard the woman's voice
saying, "Your name looks familiar. Are you a writer?"

Caught off-guard in a whole new way, I sheepishly responded, "Yes."

She asked whether I wrote for a particular blog, and I said, "Yes, how
did you know?"

"I just subscribed to it yesterday," she told me.

Looking back on that moment reminds me a bit of today's scripture. We are examples wherever we go. Even when things don't go the way we planned (sometimes in very embarrassing ways), we can still lead others to God in every kind of situation.

LET'S PRAY: "Father God, thank You for the reminder to live life in You. I know that I belong to You, and I want You to be my greatest treasure and delight. Thank You, Lord, for this awareness and love for You that never dies out but burns with great passion. In Jesus's name, amen."

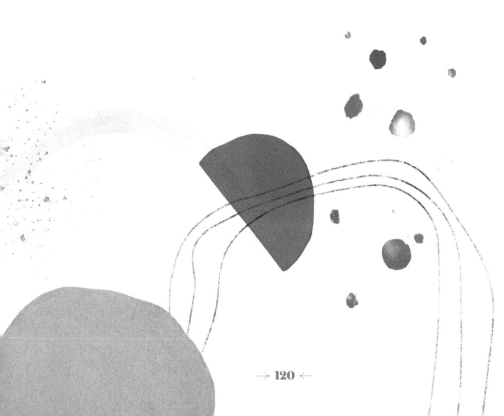

False Responsibility

Give all your worries and cares to God,
for he cares about you. → 1 Peter 5:7

Caring for others is beautiful—but to what extent? When we take someone else's burdens as our own, it may seem noble, but it could also mean we're acting as though we have the power to do something that only God can do. If we don't have the power to shoulder our own burdens without God, what makes us think we can do it for others? Sometimes we want so badly to help others that we try to hold on to their burdens and cares for them. This false sense of responsibility is dangerous because it ignores who God really is (unless of course He has called us to help in this specific instance). It's as if we're saying, "God doesn't care for you, so I'll step in and take care of you instead." Of course we know that's not true, but our belief is not seen in what we know; it's seen through our actions.

Let this be a reminder that God wants your burdens and others'. He is not afraid of them. He actually invites you to let it all out. Instead of saying with our actions, "This is something I must take care of," let us run to Him on other people's behalf.

LET'S TALK: Do you try to solve other people's problems for them? Why do you think it's so easy to fall into that trap? How can you help others bring their problems to the Lord instead of to you?

I Am So Sorry

Make allowance for each other's faults,
and forgive anyone who offends you.
Remember, the Lord forgave you, so you
must forgive others. → Colossians 3:13

As I opened my eyes one morning, I thought of a young woman whom I hadn't seen for a very long time. I had discipled her, but it ended badly due to my own immaturity after I willingly and eagerly listened to ungodly counsel.

As I saw her face in my mind, I knew the Lord wanted me to contact her. I looked through my phone and found her number—still there after all those years, but blocked. In that moment, I just followed the leading of God's love.

I nervously unblocked and texted her, unsure if it was even still her number. She texted back within minutes: "Wow! What a surprise. How are you?" I realized this meant she still had my phone number as well—and it wasn't blocked.

After a few messages back and forth, I asked whether I could call her. As we spoke on the phone, I knew not to make any excuses but to simply apologize. I let her know there was no excuse for my actions, absolutely none, and she kindly and genuinely forgave me.

She told me that after I had abruptly cut her off, she'd still chosen to grow closer to Jesus. She had read her Bible from cover to cover in three months and just craved God through the hurt. She had thrived in the Lord in spite of my and other people's doings.

It was a moment that pointed me to God and today's scripture. She was someone I had once tried to disciple, and yet in that moment, the Holy Spirit was discipling me through her. He allowed His forgiveness to flow into me, teaching me about the beauty of God's love and forgiveness.

LET'S PRAY: Today, go before the Father and lift the one who has hurt you to say, "Thank You, Lord, for ministering to this person. Go extravagantly douse them with Your love, Father. Let it be done according to the eternally vast riches of generosity that You have placed on my own life. In Jesus's name, amen."

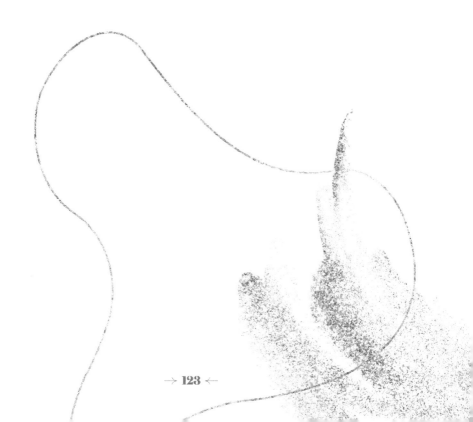

What Is Today's Assignment?

I brought glory to you here on earth by
completing the work you gave me to do.
→ John 17:4

What will attempt to distract us today from our assignment of focusing on God's greatness? What will attempt to steal our reliance and trust in God? I'm using the word "attempt" for a reason: Our trust in God can't be stolen . . . but it can be put down. And what we don't use, we often unintentionally abandon.

So today, let's abandon doubt instead of trust, and let's violently embrace God's love that is roaring within us. This roar helps us be aware of His joy that strengthens us when we're sad and His patience that causes us to lean on Him while we wait. Staying fixed on Him is part of our assignment as we bring His message out into the mission field. And our mission fields include our spouses, children, coworkers, neighbors, people who drive us crazy, people we don't know, and even ourselves!

LET'S TALK: Opportunities are around us all day long. Sometimes we don't recognize them because we have a different idea of what opportunity looks like, but that's a distraction trying to get us to fail our assignment. What was an opportunity to show God's love that you almost missed? How can you be on the lookout for these opportunities today?

Gratitude Saves Your Life

Enter into his gates with thanksgiving;
go into his courts with praise. Give thanks to
him and praise his name. For the Lord is good.
His unfailing love continues forever, and his
faithfulness continues to each generation.
→ Psalm 100:4–5

Complaining is a form of forgetting. We do it when we fail to remember all that God has done for us. In contrast, a grateful heart activates the power of God within us. Gratitude comes from a place of intentionally remembering and recounting what our amazing God has done and is continuing to do. Gratitude causes us to *count* our blessings rather than *discount* them, which puts us in a position of humility, not pride.

Along the journey, God wants us to remember all that He has done so we don't forget. We're supposed to live out our days in Him. This helps us remember to truly focus on Him who is the journey, the path, the destiny, the way. God is amazing, and just living out the story of His unfolding grace is cause to be grateful. Minister to Him by simply saying, "Thank You." And even that is not really for Him as much as it is for us, to stir the power of remembering all that He has done.

LET'S TALK: List three things about who God is that you're grateful for. What is it that causes you to remember His goodness? In every part of your life, as you look back, do you see Him in the midst of the hard and the difficult?

A Minefield of Prayer Warriors

Bless those who curse you. Pray for those who hurt you. → Luke 6:28

When I first heard my daughter was being made fun of, my claws came out—but it turned out she didn't need my help, because she had God's. The way she handled herself was mind-blowing. A boy tried to make fun of her for her Asian heritage, but she flipped his words to work for her and not against her.

"Wait! You think I look Asian?" she asked him.

He hesitated, then tried to get tough. "Yes!"

If this bully wasn't going to bless my daughter, she'd just find an opportunity to remind herself of who she knew she really was. "Thank you!" she said. "I've always wanted to look Asian, and no one has ever told me that before."

In that moment of insult, she responded with excitement that he'd noticed who she was. He had been waiting to feed on a negative reaction, and instead he just stood there admiring her response. True story.

Even when the enemy tries to attack us, through other people's cruelty or otherwise, we must remember that God has the last word. And other people see His word and His heart in the way we respond to them. Little does the enemy realize that when you and I experience discord or conflict, we view it as an opportunity for God to be seen in and through us by praying for those who try to hurt us. In trying to attack us, they've unknowingly walked into a minefield of prayer warriors—warriors who agree with God over their lives and want to reveal the God who is for them, not against them. We get to cover them in prayer in ways that blow them—and us—away!

LET'S PRAY: "Lord, thank You for the beauty of Your love, love that covers and rescues. Thank You, Father, for inviting us into this life to be a part of the rescue operations that are all around us. Help me lean into You to teach this approach even to my children. Thank You, Lord, for this bold way of living in You. In Jesus's name, amen."

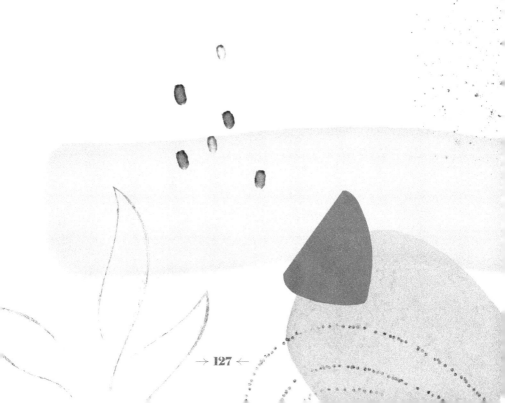

The Grapevine and the Gardener

I am the true grapevine, and my Father is the gardener. He cuts off every branch of mine that doesn't produce fruit, and he prunes the branches that do bear fruit so they will produce even more. You have already been pruned and purified by the message I have given you. Remain in me, and I will remain in you. For a branch cannot produce fruit if it is severed from the vine, and you cannot be fruit-ful unless you remain in me. → John 15:1–4

Jesus always used stories and analogies so that people would remember His teachings. Notice that everything mentioned in today's scripture has a specific part and purpose in the story: The grapevine is Jesus, the gardener is Father God, and the branch is us. God the gardener doesn't mess around. He cuts off the branches that don't bear fruit and prunes the branches that do.

A branch's fruit is evidence of what kind of plant it is. If the fruit on a branch is an apple, you know that branch is growing out of an apple tree. If the fruit is a bunch of grapes, you know it's a grapevine. If the fruit is "love, joy, peace, patience, kindness, goodness, faithfulness, gentleness, and self-control" (Galatians 5:22–23), you know it's "the true grapevine" from today's scripture. We produce God's kind of fruit by God's love in us and through us.

Notice that although they both involve cutting, there is a difference between pruning branches and cutting them off. To cut off a branch is to sever it completely, whereas pruning just cuts off small pieces of a branch so that it can produce even more fruit than before. The beautiful purpose of pruning is growth, and that only takes place when we remain on the grapevine. When we remain in Him, we see the pruning as a moment to get even closer to Him than we ever imagined. If you want to be one who produces fruit for the gardener who is God, the key is to remain intimate with Jesus by the power of the Holy Spirit.

LET'S TALK: What can you do to remain in Him? When you do remain in Him, what kind of fruit do you produce?

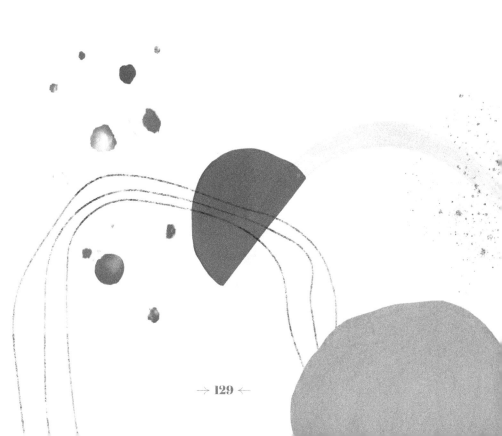

Remain to Be Fruitful

Yes, I am the vine; you are the branches. Those who remain in me, and I in them, will produce much fruit. For apart from me you can do nothing. Anyone who does not remain in me is thrown away like a useless branch and withers. Such branches are gathered into a pile to be burned. But if you remain in me and my words remain in you, you may ask for anything you want, and it will be granted! When you produce much fruit, you are my true disciples. This brings great glory to my Father.

→ John 15:5–8

Yesterday, we discussed the first part of Jesus's message about the gardener, the grapevine, and the branches. Today, we'll look at the second part. Jesus is teaching the power of remaining. Notice that He isn't emphatic about *doing*. Instead, it's all about *remaining* in Him. That's because we can't do anything godly by our own power. He makes that point clear by saying, "Apart from me you can do nothing." To be in Him *is* the ability to do—to take action out of an overabundance of holy love, not out of obligation or to fulfill expectations. The power to do anything in this life that is of eternal purpose is to just stay in Him.

The Lord wants to break any misconceptions that would cause us to attempt to do this life for His approval. He has already approved of us, and in order to do anything of Him, our only "job" is to remain in Him.

It's the opposite of how we usually comprehend things, isn't it? We so often get confused and believe we need to try as hard as we can to earn a place in the Kingdom of God. It's up to us to finally understand that remaining in Him will cause us to do more than we could ever do with our own abilities.

LET'S PRAY: "Father God, in the name of Jesus, as You are the Gardener of my life, I want to remain in Jesus, the Vine, and so I want to say thank You for Your Holy Spirit, which allows me to be a branch that produces the fruit and evidence of who You are. In Jesus's name, amen."

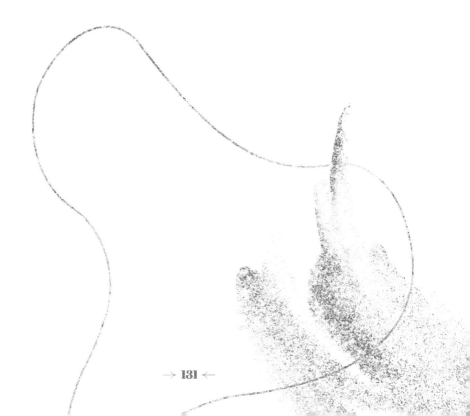

Love Remains

I have loved you even as the Father has loved me. Remain in my love. When you obey my commandments, you remain in my love, just as I obey my Father's commandments and remain in his love. I have told you these things so that you will be filled with my joy. Yes, your joy will overflow! This is my commandment: Love each other in the same way I have loved you. There is no greater love than to lay down one's life for one's friends. → John 15:9–13

Today's scripture follows the passages we've read over the last two days. These verses are so simple, yet so profound. Jesus loves us even as the Father has loved Him. As He remains in His Father, we get to remain in Jesus. When we obey the Lord, we remain in His love, just as He has remained in His Father's love.

Verse 11 reveals that the purpose of remaining in His love is to be filled with His joy, which doesn't just fill us up but actually overflows. Have you noticed the power of what Jesus wants us to do? He knows that when we remain in the One who is our Source, we become a living example for all to see. People will ask, "How are you so overflowing with joy, when everything around you is difficult and hard?" "How are you so kind to them, when they were difficult and unkind to you?" These are the moments that matter. These are the opportunities to reveal the purpose of God's extravagant love. As Jesus said, "There is no greater love than to lay down one's life for one's friends."

As He said these things, Jesus was about to display the greatest moment of pruning by going to the cross of Calvary to display the great love of the Father. The only way He could do such a feat was to remain in the Father, and in doing so, He overflowed with joy while on earth. He was the living example that is to be not just admired but also emulated.

LET'S PRAY: "Father God, as You are the Gardener of my life, I want to remain in Your love. The great love that You displayed on the cross was the greatest example of pruning. Help me see the difficulties of life as an opportunity for You to be seen so that others will want to be as a branch that remains in You, producing much fruit of Your great love. In Jesus's name, amen."

On Top and Never at the Bottom

If you listen to these commands of the Lord
your God that I am giving you today, and
if you carefully obey them, the Lord will
make you the head and not the tail, and you
will always be on top and never at the bottom.
→ Deuteronomy 28:13

I was having a hard day, but I knew I couldn't settle for that perspective. My daughter and I often remind ourselves how there are two ways to look at hardship. The first way is to see it as defeat, looking only at how the enemy is attacking us. We can feel exhausted from constantly battling the enemy and trying to anticipate what obstacles we'll face next.

The second way is to see hardship not just from a positive perspective but from *God's* perspective, by reading God's Word. Then we start to see hardship as something else, something more like an opportunity for God to be seen. It's seeing the situation not as a battle but as a victory that our God has already won. So many times, we waste our energy struggling to handle problems on our own, when God is there the entire time. With this perspective, we can stop worrying about what the enemy is up to and instead declare, "I can't wait to see what God is about to do next!"

LET'S TALK: How are you seeing your situation? From on top or at the bottom? Today, don't just shift perspective; shift your focus and gaze on God, as He is beyond worthy to be praised!

Heart Check

The human heart is the most deceitful of all things, and desperately wicked. Who really knows how bad it is? But I, the Lord, search all hearts and examine secret motives. I give all people their due rewards, according to what their actions deserve. → Jeremiah 17:9–10

Have you ever had one of those convicting, heart-checking moments? One of those revelations that seem to come out of nowhere and cause you to gasp and maybe even say out loud, "What? No!"

I had one of those recently. I had been going along, thinking I was loving people with God's love. But I was shocked to realize that I was "loving" people for what they could do for me and how they made me feel, rather than befriending them because I was simply honored to be their friend. The reality of my selfish motives stunned me.

I don't know how you've responded to these moments, but I found that wake-up call troubling, to say the least. I just sat down before the Lord and felt so sorry. In the Spirit, He lifted my head and gently showed me how many of us in the world have gone into relationships with others and even Him under false pretenses like these. If we don't like the way someone makes us feel because we didn't get our way, then we want to leave. We make it about us and what we want instead of considering the other person as well. To understand this reality was cause for a transformation of the heart—my heart in exchange for God's.

Though moments like these may feel awful at first, I soon rejoiced as I was freed by the power of the Holy Spirit. It's incredibly kind of God's loving Spirit to keep my motives in check. When I'm doing things to please myself, He reminds me to do things to please Him—things that woo others to Himself.

TRY THIS TODAY: As you go through your day today, stop at regular intervals, think about what you're doing, and simply surrender your motives to God. Try saying something like "Lord, I do this for You. Thank You, for what could have seemed like a chore, I now do for You, to please You. In Jesus's name, amen."

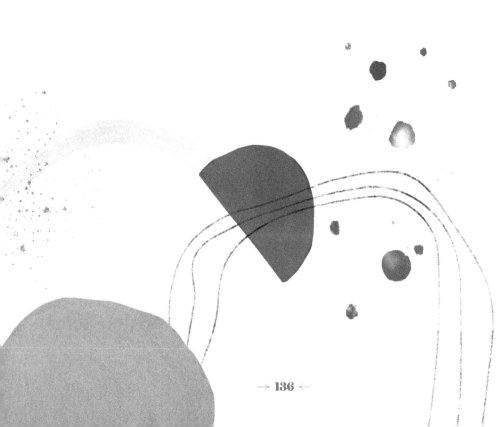

Divine Appointments

Don't worry about anything; instead, pray about everything. Tell God what you need, and thank him for all he has done. Then you will experience God's peace, which exceeds anything we can understand. → Philippians 4:6–7

Seasons pass filled with memorable moments. Some of them cause laughter, some cause tears, and others fuel worries and fears. Yet all the while, God makes Himself available at every moment, beckoning us to draw near. Each of those moments is like a rolled-up scroll filled with lessons to be learned. If we take the time to unroll it and read closely, we can learn those lessons.

I have been learning that when I consider some event a disappointment, an interruption, or an attack, it's actually an opportunity for me to see abundance instead of lack. It's a chance for me to see the miraculous ways God moves instead of seeing the glass half-empty. But to see it that way, I have to use one of the most powerful tools that exists: gratitude.

Gratitude changes your perspective as your awareness of the peace of God causes crooked things to be made straight. Being grateful softens your heart so you can experience things in a whole new way. When we finally reach for that tool, it allows us to effortlessly praise God so that we recognize Him no matter what we're going through. Gratitude brings us to our knees in awe of Him, His splendor, and His majesty.

Today's scripture reminds me to listen to how the Holy Spirit wants me to see the way He takes my disappointments and makes them into divine appointments with Him. Divine appointments to see His character of unending, unparalleled excellence, which makes the most reliable human being on Earth look reckless in comparison to Him.

LET'S TALK: Today, let's love people because He does and it's only His doing through us. As you focus on God through the scripture of Philippians 4:6–7, think about Bob Goff. He says "Give away love freely. We're rivers, not reservoirs." A bestselling author, philanthropist, and inspirational speaker, Goff believes life is meant for us to live in grace and walk in love. Think about this life in Christ as you consider Goff's words.

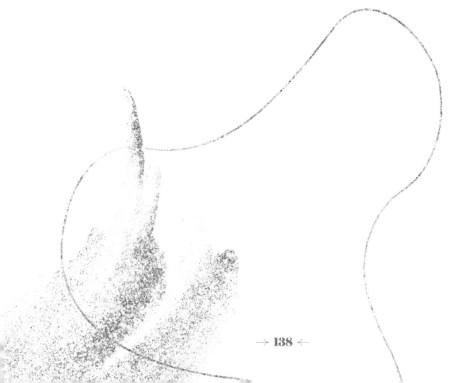

No Condemnation

So now there is no condemnation for those who belong to Christ Jesus. → Romans 8:1

For far too long, I thought that if I micromanaged, hovered, and constantly bossed my kids around, I would help them grow. But the only thing that grew was my pride in showing the world that I was in control. Although it may have seemed orderly and intentional, my idea of perfection was based more on how people perceived us than on the greater good of my children. To anyone who saw the situation for what it was, it was clear I didn't trust my children to flourish on their own.

Then, one day, I had an aha moment. I saw in my heart, like a vision, a team of tired, beaten-down people, not stirring in prosperity and creativity. I realized this team of people was what I was producing. They were unmotivated, on edge, and held back from finding out who they really were.

Then, I imagined the same team, refreshed because their coach or leader had had a change of heart. They were now seen as valuable and treasured. They were being led with encouragement as their leader pointed out their strengths, even in the midst of their weaknesses and mistakes.

I asked myself, "How does God lead me?" He doesn't condemn me; instead, He encourages me to trust Him as I cling to Him. He allows me to appreciate every moment, whether it's a victory or what seems like a defeat. Each moment is truly a classroom for God to show us who He is and why it's better to trust Him than to trust ourselves, to allow even our failures to become a win in Him. There was no shame over me—it was just a clarion call to get up in Christ and lean into Him to lead my children more like He leads me.

LET'S TALK: Whom or what are you trying to control? You can relinquish that control by surrendering it all to Him.

Who Is Writing Your Story?

You saw me before I was born. Every day of my life was recorded in your book. Every moment was laid out before a single day had passed.
→ Psalm 139:16

Often when I've prayed, I've done so from a place of fear. A fear of loss, a fear of the future, a fear of the "goings-on" of life not going the way I had hoped or wanted. Today, let's not pray from a place of fear. Let's proclaim that we know whom we're praying to. Once we remember that, doubt has to go. God is the author of our lives. He already knows about the troubles to come, and He has already written the plans to overcome them—plans for hope and a good future.

Trouble has been the main character in far too many chapters in the lives we have written for ourselves. But God has His own story. Isn't it amazing how He is always truly the main character of our stories? In fact, He must be the main everything. He must be the setting, the hero, the beginning, the middle, and the end. Let's be in awe of Him today, as we get to live because He authored us to be a part of His story—not the other way around.

LET'S PRAY: "God! Please write my life. Lord, have Your way as I cling to You and get to know who You are as the Author and the Finisher of my faith. In Jesus's name, amen."

In the Midst of a Crushed Spirit

The human spirit can endure a sick body,
but who can bear a crushed spirit?
→ Proverbs 18:14

I felt the gentle yet piercing prompt: "Call her now."

"I'll do it tomorrow," I told myself. "It's too late in the evening now."
I tried to reason the urge away, but within moments, it was as though
I couldn't help but obey. I picked up the phone. My friend's husband
of 40 years had just passed away, and I knew she needed support,
no matter how nervous I was about giving it. As the phone rang,
I thought, *What if I don't know what to say? What if I say something
wrong and make everything worse?*

When the call went to voicemail, I sighed in relief. I had given it my
best shot. It wasn't my fault no one had answered.

But my relief was interrupted by the ringing of my phone. It was my
friend, calling me back. Taking a deep breath, I answered and heard
her voice, full of grief yet covered in grace—a contrast that revealed
God was there in the midst of despair and questioning.

As we began to talk, the Holy Spirit let me hear Him through my
friend. We cried, laughed, and reminisced about her beautiful husband, who was drenched with God's love. The void she felt now that
he was gone was so deep that she knew only God could ever fill it. She
had moments of despair in which there seemed to be no evidence
that God was near. Yet, she told me, in one of those moments, she

received a text from a friend that said, "Breathe in YAH and breathe out WEH" (referring to Yahweh, one of the biblical names of God).

May we all find strength in that friend's suggestion, as we breathe the awareness of God Himself in and out.

LET'S TALK: In moments of despair—your own or someone else's—how have you seen God be an ever-present help in time of need? What happened to you and your heart after you experienced this?

Diagnostic Test

Dear friends, don't be surprised at the fiery
trials you are going through . . . Instead,
be very glad—for these trials make you
partners with Christ in his suffering, so that
you will have the wonderful joy of seeing his
glory when it is revealed to all the world.
→ 1 Peter 4:12–13

Have you ever tested your smoke alarm to see whether it works?
You're supposed to check the alarm from time to time to ensure that
when it matters most, the alarm will be in working order.

Like a smoke alarm, I too am an instrument—an instrument of praise
and faith. There are moments ("fiery trials," as today's scripture calls
them) that test my ability to stand in my rightful place in Christ Jesus,
and I've malfunctioned a few more times than I would've hoped. But
instead of letting me stay defeated, the Holy Spirit has caused joy
in the Lord to arise in me. This joy is my signal to recharge my bat-
teries by running to the Father whose strength is made perfect in
my weakness.

Think about it. Trials are a powerful "diagnostic test" that reveal
whether we're operating in fear or in faith. When we're operating in
fear, we end up attempting to control our situations, and even other
people, on our own. Yet I am beginning—yes, I said *beginning*—to
learn that the trials and tests that come are only to make sure our
faith is in God and not in ourselves or anyone else. His strength is
glorified in overcoming our weakness.

LET'S PRAY: "Father God, in the name of Jesus, You are my God. Your grace that empowers me to rise above sin and shame allows me to make a glorious spectacle of Your splendor within my family and beyond. Thank You, Lord, for the trials that show You can overcome my weakness so that the people around me will see You and Your goodness more clearly. In Jesus's name, amen."

I Want Nature to Join My Praise

The heavens proclaim the glory of God. The skies display his craftsmanship. → Psalm 19:1

As I opened the doors to my backyard and was greeted by the first breath of the day, I was filled with great awe. Provoked by nature's declarations of divine glory, I felt a desire to be in deep, holy trepidation of our mighty God! Coming back inside, I grabbed my worn and torn Bible and opened it up to find a simple yet profound scripture I had previously highlighted. It was that moment in Luke 19:40 when the Pharisees pretend to be piously concerned that people were praising Jesus instead of God, and He replies that even if people kept quiet, "the stones along the road would burst into cheers!"

That reminded me of today's scripture and led me to say, "Lord, whether I praise You or not, nature itself will proclaim who You are. But I don't want nature to have to replace my voice. Instead, I want nature to echo my own praises to God. I want all of nature to be encouraged by my awe of the King of Glory."

LET'S PRAY: "Father God, I know You are the only One I can be in awe of. You are so amazing, You are so good, and You are more than worthy to be praised in every moment of my life on Earth. In Jesus's name, amen."

Casting the Stone Meets the Cornerstone

You were cleansed from your sins when you obeyed the truth, so now you must show sincere love to each other as brothers and sisters. Love each other deeply with all your heart. → 1 Peter 1:22

The profound command in today's scripture leads me back to the woman who was caught in the act of adultery. Think about it—caught in the very act itself! She might even have been naked as she was dragged in front of many judgmental onlookers. Yet Jesus seemed to pause time as He silenced the accusers with that incredible statement that is still remembered 2,000 years later: "Let him who is without sin among you be the first to throw a stone at her" (John 8:7, ESV).

For everyone in that scene, the moment had to cause a life-altering paradigm shift. The one person present who could have cast those stones at her was the one who chose to protect her instead. The love of God manifested upon the earth like no one had ever seen or imagined.

There He was, standing before all of them, the greatest stone of all—"the stone that the builders rejected" that had "now become the cornerstone" (Matthew 21:42). Instead of casting a stone, He cast Himself over her as her stronghold, not to hurt her but to reveal God's goodness so He could then say, "Go and sin no more" (John 8:11).

He addressed the sin, but He also empowered her with His goodness so that she could lead a lifestyle of repentance, never turning back to her sin and instead following Jesus all the days of her life.

LET'S TALK: Are you like that woman—so overwhelmed by His love that you can't help but love others with the love you've freely received from Him? When we awaken to Him, we get to become a display of His glory by His mighty power.

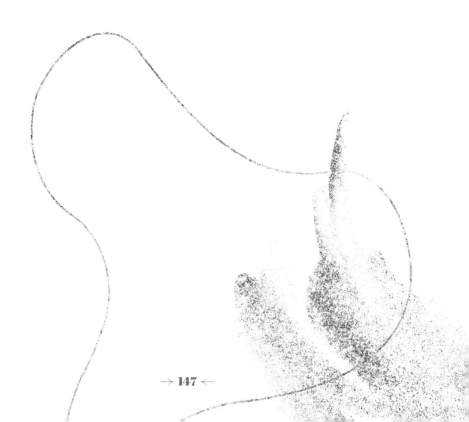

There's Beauty in Rejection

Even if my father and mother abandon me, the Lord will hold me close. → Psalm 27:10

There's beauty in rejection? Oh yes! Think of all the times you've been rejected; you now get to see these as "God opportunities." It's easier said than done, yet I sit here and wonder, "What if I allowed rejection to be the arrow that directs me to the Father?"

Through the twists and turns, the gains and losses, from rejection to acceptance, from health to sickness, I am learning I must choose how I see this life. Life may seem like it's "us against the world," but in reality, we are simply in the world, not of it. The key to reframing rejection is not to live in denial but to remember you're a sojourner in this life, not a permanent resident. As today's scripture reminds us, no matter how painful rejection might be here on earth, the Lord will hold us close. We get to see life in Christ as an opportunity to bless those who have rejected us and thank God we had them on our journey. That's how we release them and see the beauty in rejection.

LET'S PRAY: "Father God, thank You for the reminder that I cannot be rejected by a temporary world that has never accepted me. I want to be in awe of Your acceptance much more than someone else's rejection. Thank You for this sweet reminder from Your Word. In Jesus's name, amen."

The Only One in the World

O Lord, you have examined my heart and know everything about me. You know when I sit down or stand up. You know my thoughts even when I'm far away . . . You know everything I do. You know what I am going to say even before I say it, Lord. → Psalm 139:1–4

As I write these words, there's an image I can't get out of my thoughts. I see a woman who has no specific facial characteristics and no specific skin tone, yet she's not just a silhouette. Somehow, I just know this woman represents every woman. And when I think of her, I hear God saying, "I see her; I see you."

What a reminder from God Himself. His eyes don't just pass over you as He looks across a crowd. He takes notice of you as though you're the only one in the world. You are God's love letter to this world; allow His pen to write upon your heart so that you begin loving yourself as He intended. Let's love with His eternal love over anyone and everyone we encounter. He wants to meet each one of those people right where they are.

LET'S PRAY: "Father God, I've got to know You so that I can truly perceive who You are and what You see. The depths of keen vision within people are hidden from us until we see from where You are. Father God, thank You for this revelation—now let it be the way I live. In Jesus's name, amen."

The Heart of Worship

You will show me the way of life,
granting me the joy of your presence and
the pleasures of living with you forever.
→ Psalm 16:11

While watching a news story about a sports event that occurred without crowds due to safety measures during the COVID-19 pandemic, I was in awe of how the athletes performed. Though there were no spectators, they played as though the stadium were packed. It revealed their passion for the game, no matter who was or wasn't there.

It reminded me of the song "The Heart of Worship" by Matt Redman. If you've heard it, you know it's about ignoring all the accoutrements that we as humans bring to worship and simply focusing on the Lord. These athletes didn't have any cheering fans or the other usual game-day trappings, but that only revealed how pure their love of the sport was.

It was a moment in which I saw a glimpse of the difference between the temporal and eternal perspectives. In that very moment, I went to my phone and played the song, thinking about getting to a place where even when no one is watching us, we know He is there.

LET'S PRAY: "Father God, every moment is another moment to keep being aware of You with my heart of worship. The things that have unknowingly taken residence upon the throne of my heart must bow to You today. I surrender my moments today as I desire to everyday. In Jesus's name, amen."

Avalanche

We destroy every proud obstacle that
keeps people from knowing God. We capture
their rebellious thoughts and teach them
to obey Christ. → 2 Corinthians 10:5

I woke up with a grateful heart. Yet within moments, I had hurried
myself and skipped over the time I use to surrender my day to the
Lord and hear the Lord speak. As I got ready for the day, my mind
went from being grateful to being whisked away by random worries
that grew from snowflakes into avalanches within minutes.

Reminders of today's scripture rolled through my heart, yet the pride
of not wanting to bend caused me to bask in despair. Finally, the Word
penetrated my heart, after I asked myself a question: "Does this thing
I'm upset about even matter?" The answer was an obvious "No!"
God's mighty love was staring right at me, beckoning me to be still and
know that He is God. That moment awakened me to turn my attention
and affections toward God and God alone. It caused me to melt the
self-destructive avalanche of worry into a flood of praises to God.

TRY THIS TODAY: Is there something you've allowed to take
your affections away from God? Focus on His goodness, and He
will highlight it as you worship Him in whatever you're doing in this
moment. Simply say with a repentant heart, "Thank You for Your forgiveness, Lord." And now continue dwelling in Him, and watch your
actions and motives shift.

We Keep Going

The godly may trip seven times, but they will get up again. But one disaster is enough to overthrow the wicked. → Proverbs 24:16

I had been working on putting a dresser together for over five hours. Panel A, slot B, Allen wrench. Some not-so-nice words had traveled from my mouth more often than I would like to admit.

I started to get excited as I finally neared the finish line, when, to my surprise, I realized I had messed up early in the process. I hadn't lined up certain holes on one of the panels correctly, and now, at the very end of the process, I saw that they were facing the wrong way. Now I'd have to take it apart and start all over again.

It reminds me of those moments when we think we're doing the right thing, but in the end, it turns out not to be what God wants. We can have the best intentions but still end up putting things together all wrong. Then we have to go back to the beginning and start over.

But here's what's so amazing about God: We can simply repent. As God's people, even when we "trip seven times," we are never down. We are either up or getting up as our eyes stay fixed on Him.

Here's a great reminder: When you trip and fall, it doesn't mean that you're a "mess" or a "klutz." God doesn't say, "Arise, My klutz!" Nor does He say, "Come on, you mess!" Instead, He declares, "Arise in who I am, My daughter." It's not about the mistakes; it's about the God who gives us the mercy and grace to keep going and rise above what we could never do on our own.

LET'S PRAY: "Thank You, Lord, for Your greatness. I love how You are not moved by my trips and falls. Instead, You are immovable, steady, and everlasting. In Jesus's name, amen."

Pursued to Pursue

May the words of my mouth and the
meditation of my heart be pleasing to you,
O Lord, my rock and my redeemer.
→ Psalm 19:14

Do you ever feel awe at the creativity and skill of a piece of art, without even knowing who the artist is? I am humbly reminded that this can happen with the beauty of creation. I can be in awe of the Creator's handiwork but not truly know Him. He wants us to know Him so intimately—not just know *about* Him but truly *know* Him by His Spirit.

He wants us to climb into the depths of His heart, where we will see a glimpse of His magnificent, holy face. If we do that wherever we go and whatever we do, we'll reveal His glory. We'll find opportunities to be in His creative "love story" of hope, pursuing others to woo them to their true destiny, encouraging them as they receive the kisses of God through us until they, in turn, pursue and woo.

He gives His matchless, endless, and incomprehensible love to others through us with hopeful embraces, words of encouragement, time measured not in quantity but in quality, and acts of service with a cheerful heart. These gifts from within make room for the King of Kings to enter our lives with refreshment as we pour out onto others, never running dry, revealing His royalty.

Let's continue in this intimate pursuit of our King. Let's not wait until we face tough times but do it in every moment—during our highs, lows, and mediums. Let's not just know His work, but let's know Him by the Revealer, who is the Holy Spirit revealing the Word of God in and through our lives. Dive into His Word today and watch what you explore in Him. You'll never want to do life without Him.

LET'S TALK: What is one thing you want to know about who He is? Do you want to get to a place where you never want to do life without Him? Do you want to get to a place where you don't just know Him for what He has done but desire to know Him for who He is? This is where intimacy begins.

Be Impressed

If you receive a prophet as one who speaks for God, you will be given the same reward as a prophet. And if you receive righteous people because of their righteousness, you will be given a reward like theirs. → Matthew 10:41

I think phrases like "I'm not easily impressed" need to be humbly annihilated by God's love. Why? Because I'm learning that other people—no matter who they are or what they do—all contain the supernatural beauty of God. We can receive the gifts of God that are within others with open hands. But not if we're trying to act unimpressed.

Recognizing the beautiful gifts of God in others is a simple yet profound way to make an eternal impact. Just as nature exquisitely declares the glory of God, so do other people, which I realize when I deliberately take notice. People are not meant just to be seen. They're meant to be honored and recognized as treasures, unique masterpieces, fearfully and wonderfully made by God. So today, no matter where we are or what we're doing, let's be impressed by the beauty of God within others.

LET'S PRAY: "Father God, I want to celebrate You as I celebrate others, knowing this honors You. Whether it be my family, friends, or people I'm meeting for the first time, let me be impressed over and over again. In Jesus's name, amen."

Ministering to the Heart of God

> While they were ministering to the Lord and fasting, the Holy Spirit said, "Set apart for Me Barnabas and Saul for the work to which I have called them." → Acts 13:2 (NASB)

Imagine a young man or woman whose calling is to be in ministry. This person walks the path of ministry laid out in front of them, reaching milestones and checking off boxes. But what if that's not the path that God intended? What if they're listening to the earthly voices of people who have good intentions about what "ministry" means to them but don't quite understand what it means to God?

Their hearts yearn to do good for God, and they may even seem successful from the outside. Yet on the inside, they feel empty, because they don't realize that their greatest task is to minister to the heart of God, which in turn automatically ministers to people. The Holy Spirit is whispering for you to awaken, arise, stand, walk, and run with the intention to just minister to God's heart by being an influence wherever you are—whether it's at home, at the grocery store, traveling, or anywhere else. That means expressing love with kindness, complimenting someone, and opening the door for them.

Ministering to God's heart is especially important when it comes to your children. When they're acting up, you can look them intently in the eyes and tell them how valued they are, but that what they're doing doesn't line up with who they actually are. If they're doing things that are unkind, try saying something like, "You are so kind and an incredible human being, but your actions need to line up with that now."

Ministering to God is not about what we do for a living. It's about expressing His love through our living. It's about demonstrating honor and kindness wherever you go, speaking kindly and treating others exceptionally well.

LET'S PRAY: "Lord, I'm so grateful I get to minister to and worship You. Thank You that when I'm in You, You cause my doings to be overtaken by Your grace. Thank You for being my strength, my joy, and my everything. In Jesus's name, amen."

A Great Runner

Since we believe that Christ died for all,
we also believe that we have all died to
our old life. → 2 Corinthians 5:14

I've always been a great runner. I don't mean that I'm great at getting up for early-morning jogs or registering for half-marathons; I mean that I've routinely run away from problems, people, and difficult times. I've even run to different cities, as if changing my location would help me escape my difficulties. It may have seemed like I was "getting away" at the time, but I hadn't died to my old life, which meant that my mindset wasn't transformed and the same issues kept reappearing. As long as I was still trying to protect my ego, it didn't matter where I ran to—"I" still showed up.

In this life in Christ, self cannot live in His presence. It must die so we can come alive to Jesus. Rather than running away (which never truly solves our problems), we must run toward and with Jesus. This happens by reading the love letter of God, the Bible, which renews us in our pursuit of His heart and lets us run deeper and deeper into who He is.

LET'S PRAY: "Father, I thank You for Your love. Your goodness causes me to no longer run *from* You but *to* You. It lets me turn from myself and toward You. Thank You for the ability to run not just with You but in You. In Jesus's name, amen."

Time Heals?

For I know the plans I have for you . . . They are plans for good and not for disaster, to give you a future and a hope. → Jeremiah 29:11

We often use clichés without stopping to think about whether they truly make sense or not. Who hasn't said, "Time heals"? But can you imagine telling that to a precious elderly person on their deathbed? Or what about the ruins of a city—does "time" pick up the debris? Does "time" come alongside a child who lost both parents and embrace them? Does "time" feed and clothe you when you have no resources? No. Time does nothing but bulldoze right through us.

It's what we *do* with our time that determines whether we heal or not. Spending that time with God gives us the grace to get through this life when we can't do it on our own. He is the One who gives generously. He brings healing and forgiveness to the broken and to those who have caused others to be brokenhearted. And not only does He set us free, He also teaches us how to lean on Him and stay in Him—He who is freedom.

LET'S TALK: Have you believed that time would heal you? Whether you did or not, do you desire to partner with God and allow Him to heal you? He goes beyond the confines of time and space. He is not too busy. Go to Him now. He's waiting for you.

One Step at a Time

The Lord directs the steps of the godly.
He delights in every detail of their lives.
→ Psalm 37:23

One morning, when my daughter was a teenager, I walked into her room and whispered, "Good morning."

She lay snuggled beneath the fluffy covers. With a sweet smile, she said, "Hi, Mom. I was up earlier."

"Did you get to read the Word today?" I asked with excitement.

"Yes, but I talked with Jesus more than I read." She smiled. "Mom, you need to read what God shared with me."

She handed me a piece of paper with the title "One Step at a Time" written at the top. As I read what she'd penned, I was full of awe toward God. She asked how she could help bring God to her generation and into the next one. She wrote about how it was key to take action and not be paralyzed by what-ifs and excuses for not moving forward. The lesson she had taken away from talking with Jesus was that she was learning to seek God all of her days, to see that it was something she *got* to do, not something she *had* to do. That if she had a willing heart to listen to and obey God instead of assuming she knew what He wanted, she would stay close to the Lord as He showed her the next steps, one step at a time. She wrote that if the King of Kings from the past to the present and into the future wanted to do life with her for all of her days, she was in.

I'm in, too.

LET'S TALK: Today's scripture is such a great reminder that God just wants us to be in Him. He doesn't need our help; He just wants our willingness to believe and trust Him. What are you learning today about doing this life in Christ one step at a time? How does this help you?

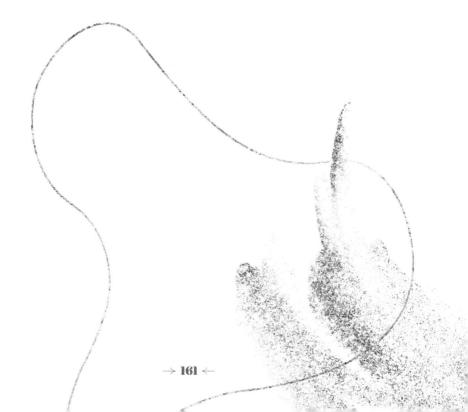

Caught in the Act

Never stop praying.
→ 1 Thessalonians 5:17

Evidence of a new day peered subtly through the windows as all creation seemed to declare God's glory. Waking up to this natural alarm clock, I was led to bless the Lord even before I was fully aware of the new day.

I looked at the time. It was 6:11 a.m., so I decided to turn to Daniel 6:11, where I found this scripture: "Then the officials went together to Daniel's house and found him praying and asking for God's help." In the Babylonian court where Daniel was situated, it was illegal to worship the true God instead of King Darius. But Daniel had been caught praying.

The story goes on from there, but there was a principle that God wanted me to take in as He highlighted that particular verse. If you're going to get caught doing anything, get caught praying.

TRY THIS TODAY: While you're in the middle of your day, take notice of the miracles in plain sight. The best way to do this is to pray without ceasing. Prayer makes you aware of the Holy Spirit who is within you. Perhaps at the end of the night, or whenever you're led, get a journal and write down the miracles of God you took notice of today. It could be the simplest thing. Write the date so that when you look back, it's a note to declare that you saw God was right there.

Rejoicing Refuge

But let all who take refuge in you rejoice; let them sing joyful praises forever. Spread your protection over them, that all who love your name may be filled with joy. → Psalm 5:11

I was out having fun with some girlfriends when, seemingly at random, I said, "When I laugh, I roar. When I cry, it pours. And when I sleep, I snore." We all laughed so hard. There's something about a contagious laugh that reminds me to live with gratitude and to actively encourage others. That's what I want to do in this life—to be known for the contagious joy of the Lord that brings strength and heals.

We haven't even tapped into the depths of God's power within us waiting to burst forth. Can you imagine if the levees of unbelief broke and allowed the living water to overflow out of us, onto us and others? This ongoing experience is for others to share as well. The gifts that flow in us are never about saying, "Look what I have . . . and look what you don't have." They're truly about saying, "Look what I have, and you can have it, too!"

LET'S TALK: Laughter, joy, compassion, and kindness defy depression and negativity. Joy is to negativity as light is to darkness. What are you going to do today that releases the evidence of God's strength?

A Different Angle

Little children, you are from God
and have overcome them, for he who
is in you is greater than he who is
in the world. → 1 John 4:4 (ESV)

I was driving out of a parking lot onto a busy road when I was startled to see a man hanging by his fingertips off the back of a large truck. I started to panic. His life was in danger! But as traffic moved forward, my view of the man changed, and I realized he was actually just riding a motorcycle with very high handlebars that had blended in with the background. I laugh as I remember that moment, but it's a great reminder that sometimes we need to see things from a different angle. My brain had sent me a false message about this man that seemed so believable, but a change in perspective revealed that it was an illusion.

So it is in our lives with God. Many times, when we're going through stressful situations, we believe things that aren't really true and start to panic. But when we remain in Jesus, then our thinking continually comes into alignment with His, and we can see the world and His love for us more clearly.

TRY THIS TODAY: Today, work on viewing every obstacle as an opportunity to find Jesus in every given situation. At the end of the day, come back to God and ask Him to go with you through your recollections of the day. Watch how He opens your spiritual eyes to see Him.

From Broken to Beautiful

He has sent me to tell those who mourn that the time of the Lord's favor has come . . . To all who mourn in Israel, he will give a crown of beauty for ashes, a joyous blessing instead of mourning, festive praise instead of despair. → Isaiah 61:2–3

The glass bottle shattered, and olive oil spilled everywhere. What a waste of my oil, not to mention my time! Or maybe it was a lesson in the making. Because that's when I saw the raw, naked truth of God in that broken vessel. It was as though I could hear the whisper of the Spirit: "I waste nothing. What you see as broken, I have already restored. I am restorer, rebuilder, and redeemer."

In that moment, I took a different view of the broken glass I had to clean up. In fact, the light reflecting off the spilled oil on the floor was oddly beautiful. It was as though I was hearing the whisper of the Holy Spirit saying, "The rich vastness of heaven is what is released when you allow your brokenness to reveal My glory."

I want to be very clear on this: If we're broken because of self-inflicted wounds, then let's quickly repent and ask God to help us live for Him. In no way do I ignorantly invite pain. But when pain does come, will I allow myself to recognize the majestic glory of God, which is evidence that He is right there?

Don't focus on *not* sinning—instead, focus on the One who gives life, and watch the longing to sin dissipate as you become ever more deeply in awe of God. More than anything, recognizing the oil of heaven in the midst of our unforeseen broken glass allows us to be aware of our transition from broken to beautiful.

LET'S TALK: What in your life that seemed to be a waste is now revealed as a triumphant reminder of God's grace? Let's allow His oil to permeate us with supernatural joy so that every time we're tempted to waver and shake, we hear and see Him in the midst.

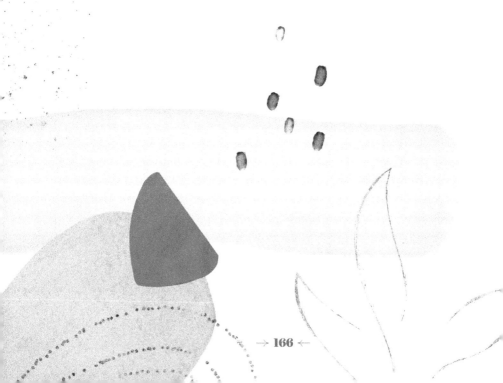

Traces of Joy

For the despondent, every day brings trouble;
for the happy heart, life is a continual feast.
→ Proverbs 15:15

One day, as I was tidying up the house in a needless hurry, a wave of pondering and wondering came over me and I sat down. Out of nowhere, I was reminded of how many times I had walked up those stairs, through that hallway, into those bedrooms. I thought of the prayers I'd whispered, the worries that had attempted to grip my thoughts, and the things that had distracted me from the greatness of God. I imagined all those moments slipping through my grasp as seconds turned into minutes, minutes into hours, hours into days, days into weeks, and weeks into years.

Yet I also remembered the moments when I was intentionally joyful. The years of training to look for God in moments of frustration and irritation as well as joy. Even when I didn't feel it at first, I was able to enjoy those moments in the Lord.

I looked at the dust on the baseboards, physical evidence left behind by time. I wondered what kind of evidence I was leaving behind as I went through life. Did I leave traces of faith or fear? Despair or joy?

As I asked myself these questions, I heard in my heart the most important question of all: "Do you see Me in the midst?" Today's scripture is such a beautiful reminder to take this very moment and look for evidence of God with a happy heart, remembering that this life in Christ is a continual feast.

LET'S TALK: What passing moments of your day have tried to steal your affections from the "right now" with God? Are there things that you feel you must put on pause because of decisions that need to be made? Perhaps today is the day you decide to just jump in with God and do whatever He has asked of you. It's the one step you get to take, and then He takes it from there. Even if that step is writing down what He told you, then do that. Lift that writing up to the Lord and just say, "Lord, I surrender even this to You. Have Your way."

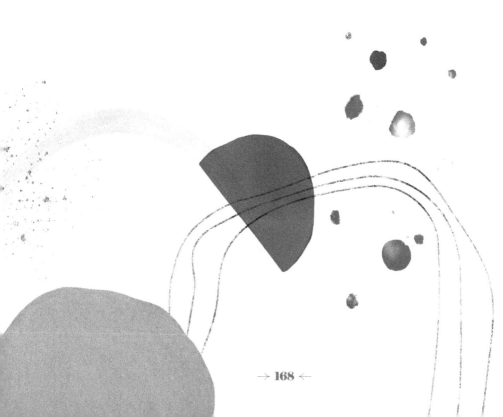

Trafficked

No, O people, the Lord has told you what is
good, and this is what He requires of you:
to do what is right, to love mercy, and to walk
humbly with your God. → Micah 6:8

Think about this: When we are hurt, wrongfully accused, or taken advantage of, in Christ's strength we are able to see ourselves not as victims but as intercessors. We get to be prayer warriors for those who have wronged us and plead that their lives no longer be "trafficked" by the enemy. We are able to bless those who wrongfully accuse us for a heavenly purpose, so that they will step out of the courtroom of the accuser—for the judgment that will come upon them if we don't intercede for them could be catastrophic.

When people think they're taking advantage of us, it's actually our opportunity to get the last word with God and do good for them. This excites me, because we get to be the ones who give that moment to the Lord as a form of worship. It's a sown seed, and we can surely expect a harvest of souls for God's Kingdom.

When you begin to see these situations as sowing moments, you realize it's impossible for someone to truly take advantage of you, because you'll just give that moment to God. Through our actions we reveal the sign, wonder, and miracle of God's goodness, which leads people to repentance so they can be made right with God. It's about seeing people come out from the kingdom of darkness into God's glorious light!

LET'S PRAY: "Father God, thank You for the ability to be Your light in the darkness. I am so grateful that by Your grace and power I get to be an intercessor. Even if the enemy sends someone my way, he sent them to the wrong place, because they just stepped into the camp of an intercessor who will pray them into Your Kingdom. May they be changed forever, from generation to generation. In Jesus's name, amen."

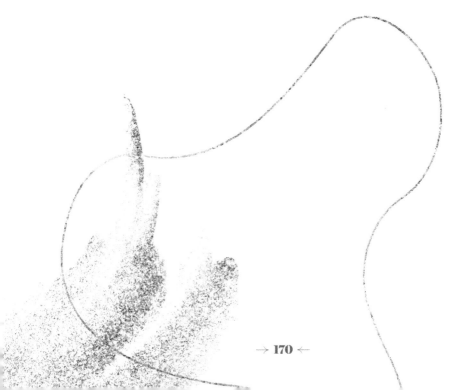

What You're About to Do

I pray that God, the source of hope,
will fill you completely with joy and peace
because you trust in him. Then you will overflow with confident hope through the power
of the Holy Spirit. → Romans 15:13

I was having one of those moments when I was just waiting to see what else could go wrong. But then I heard the Holy Spirit's whisper telling me to say, "Lord! I am so excited to see what You are about to do—the very thing that You have planned and purposed from long ago!" And with His prompting, my perspective suddenly shifted. It went from expecting mayhem to being aware of the miracle-working power of Almighty God.

Isn't that amazing? There are moments when we fear to believe God because of our experiences with disappointment. However, we can take those disappointments and turn them into opportunities to fix our eyes on God, who is our happening, our hope, and our dream come true.

LET'S PRAY: "Lord, what have You planned? I want to be in awe of You, no matter my circumstances. I want my circumstances to have no weight in comparison to Your glory. You are my proper perspective. In Jesus's name, amen."

Rescue, Protect, Cover

For he will rescue you from every trap and protect you from deadly disease. He will cover you with his feathers. He will shelter you with his wings. His faithful promises are your armor and protection. Do not be afraid of the terrors of the night, nor the arrow that flies in the day.
→ Psalm 91:3–5

Many years ago, my daughter, Tristin, was paralyzed by fear during tornado season. At the time, we lived in the Midwest, and one of the towns near us, with a population of about 2,000 people, was almost annihilated by a tornado. From then on, even a light rainfall would cause her to cry, and it was almost impossible to comfort her.

As a family, we had recently learned about the power of God as revealed in Psalm 91. So my husband and I sat Tristin down at the dining table and told her about the power of God and how He protects us. We gave her the Bible and read the promises of God over her life. She was only in first grade at the time, and she surprised us by memorizing the entire chapter. She started to speak it whenever she saw the sky turn gray or raindrops begin to fall.

One evening, my husband had the radio going, since we knew there were storms brewing. I myself was starting to give in to fear, and I didn't want Tristin listening. As my husband and I went around the house gathering the things we needed to take shelter, we came back into our room and found the Bible opened to none other than Psalm 91. Tristin trusted the Word of God so much that she'd placed it on the windowsill. We couldn't find her for a few minutes. It turned out she was praying. She faced God in the midst of her fear and let His Word rule in her heart.

Do you know that when we listened to the radio that night, we learned that the tornado that had been traveling straight for us had lifted up, changed direction, and lost momentum? Tristin literally witnessed God's miracle. She is now 20 years old, and she actually loves rainstorms, just as she continues to practice leaning into God as her rescuer, shelter, and protector. It's not just about knowing God rescues her; it's about knowing that even if something happened, if she believed in God, she would lose nothing but gain everything.

TRY THIS TODAY: Get to know God even more through Psalm 91. He isn't too busy for you. He's waiting. Is there an area of your life that paralyzes you with fear? Surrender it to God at this very moment and thank Him for who He is: Father, protective covering, and steadfast shelter.

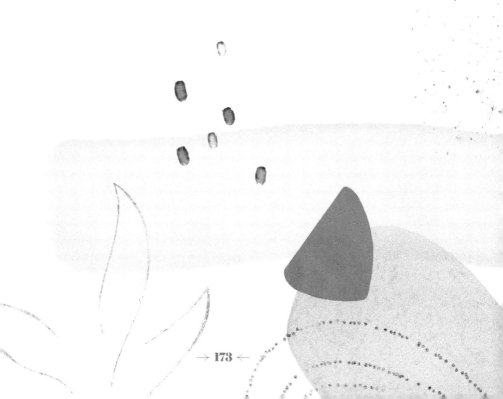

Zooming In

The Lord is watching everywhere, keeping
his eye on both the evil and the good.
→ Proverbs 15:3

Have you ever spent time looking at Google Maps? You can start with
a view of Earth from space and then zoom in closer and closer. If you
keep zooming, you'll start seeing continents, countries, and cities.
Eventually, you can zoom in so close that you can see the front door of
your house.

The same kind of zooming happens with prayer. For instance, when
you pray for your city, what do you imagine? When I pray over Austin,
Texas, where I live, I zoom out: I see the silhouette of the city's sky-
scrapers, slow-moving cars in major traffic, and sidewalks filled with
groups of people. But we can't stay zoomed out forever.

One day at a store, a cashier was rude to me. My first reaction was "I'll
show you rude!" But my train of thought was interrupted by an image
in my mind's eye. I saw that distant satellite view of Earth from space,
just like on Google Maps. Then the view began to zoom in.
I saw oceans, mountains, the borders of different countries. I saw the
United States, then Texas, then the city of Austin. The view zoomed
in closer and closer, until *bam*, it stopped right at that very store,
focused on the person who stood before me.

It was as though I heard a voice in my spirit saying, "Teresa, you
prayed for the city of Austin, and I just highlighted one of its people.
What will you do with this? Will you remain offended? Will you see
this as an opportunity for My love to be seen? Will you take this
opportunity to be the light?"

LET'S TALK: Have there been times when you've taken your circumstances as a personal offense instead of looking at them from a larger perspective? Next time, don't take it personally—personally take it to the Lord.

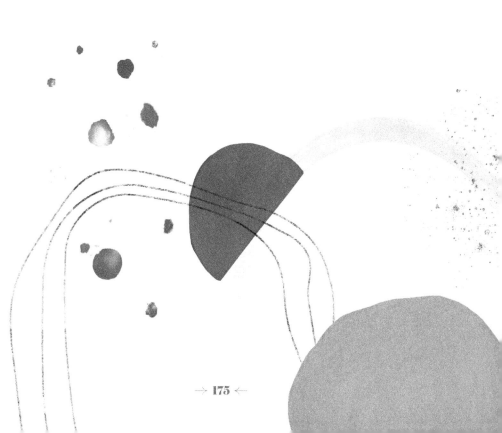

Preparation

For we are God's masterpiece. He has created us anew in Christ Jesus, so we can do the good things he planned for us long ago.
→ Ephesians 2:10

Prep time is often the lengthiest part of the cooking process—laying out all the necessary ingredients, chopping and dicing, mixing and seasoning, and of course, remembering to preheat the oven to the correct temperature. It takes a lot of time. Often, it feels like you'll never finish, and when you do, you still have to do the actual cooking! But when you step back and see that all your work created a meal ready to eat and enjoy, you realize it was all worth it.

So it is in our spiritual lives. Through our everyday moments, even when the preparation feels endless, we know that one day, we'll see a beautiful masterpiece brought together in the end. During those times when it seemed like we were chopping endless onions or feeling the intense heat of the oven, we weren't seeing the full picture. But when all the ingredients come together, the mixing, pouring, and baking will create a meal that is worth it all.

LET'S PRAY: "Father God, thank You for preparing me in who You are. Thank You for equipping me with Your Spirit to do the things that I could not do in my own strength. When I trust You even in the intense heat, I am able to flourish while pointing others forward and upward to You. In Jesus's name, amen."

Refreshment

Good news from far away is like cold water
to the thirsty. → Proverbs 25:25

On March 5, 2003, I went to bed depressed, hopeless, and pessimistic, feeling like I'd live that way for the rest of my life. I had been raised in a godly home, and yet for 10 years, I'd been a wayward daughter with no awareness of who God was or what it was like to live for Him. Every night I'd go to bed sad, and every morning I'd wake up anxious or scared. I didn't know why things were like that, but I expected that night to be no different.

Yet this time I was awakened in the morning with a gentle touch on my shoulder. I opened my eyes and turned to see who it was, but there was no one there (or so I thought). It was the first time in years that I'd woken up actually feeling peaceful.

As I got out of bed, it seemed as though I floated out of the bedroom and into the office. Closing the door behind me, I walked over to the desk and picked up the journal and pen that I had bought the day before. I took a seat on the floor in front of the futon, and as though I had done it many times before, I began writing praises to God. It was as if I heard a whisper, sweet and gentle, that said, "You will write praises to Me for the rest of your life."

This encounter happened in a moment. After 10 years of my family believing in God for my return to the Lord, it literally happened in a moment. Can you imagine how today's scripture came to life for my family? Like cold water to the thirsty indeed.

LET'S TALK: Are you believing in God for a wayward son or daughter to return? When you hear about their wayward ways, are you speaking the Word over them? If not, begin declaring the promises of God over them. Declare that the good news of the Lord is coming to your household in Jesus's name.

Hope in the Lord

We put our hope in the Lord. He is our help
and our shield. In him our hearts rejoice,
for we trust in his holy name. Let your unfailing
love surround us, Lord, for our hope is in
you alone. → Psalm 33:20–22

What I wanted more than anything else was for certain people in my
family to come to church with me. It was a constant source of stress
in my life, and I allowed it to become overwhelming and daunting.
I convinced myself that if I didn't get what I wanted, I wouldn't be
able to bear it. Even my prayers to God were guarded. I almost didn't
want to pray, because what if what I prayed for didn't happen? Then
perhaps I would believe that my prayer didn't work. Even deeper than
that, I worried: What if those family members never came to church?
I couldn't face the possibility.

But, finally, I was awakened by the truth of today's scripture, which
jolted me out of my feeling of turmoil to God Himself. This reminder
from Psalm 33 flooded me with the knowledge that "our hope is in You
alone." This transformed my mind as I realized that even when what
I'm hoping for is something good, in the end, God alone is my true
hope. No matter what's going on in my life, God is the one who's in
control. Nothing I can do could compare to the things He does.

With this realization, I went from anxiously hoping for the outcome
I wanted to experiencing the peace and hope of knowing God
and trusting His plan. In that place of hope, I can experience true
contentment—not just being content when I get what I want, but
being content in God.

LET'S TALK: What have you been hoping for? Are you placing
your hope in God? Do you know He can truly be trusted? Is there
something holding you back from truly knowing Him?

Riding Her Bike

But let patience have its perfect work, that you
may be perfect and complete, lacking nothing.
→ James 1:4 (NKJV)

When our daughter was in the fourth grade, she developed a sudden
interest in learning how to ride a bike. We were all excited for her to
experience this step along the way to adulthood. But as we drove
to the empty school parking lot where she could practice, it seemed
that the closer we got, the more anxious she became. Suddenly, the
fear of falling outweighed the excitement and fun of learning how
to ride.

We parked our truck and removed the bike from the back, but she was
hesitant to climb on. It was important to me that fear have no foothold
in her life, and I took it upon myself to make sure that she would not
be robbed of this precious milestone. My intentions were good, but
my actions were full of major impatience.

Although this moment happened years ago, my daughter still remem-
bers it to this day. From what she says, I was patient for a little bit,
gently trying to coax her onto the bike. But soon, I began showing
impatience as I yelled with everything in my being, "Tristin! Get on
that bike! We aren't leaving until you get on it!"

Yikes! In those moments, my lack of self-control revealed that
I lacked God's patience and love with my precious daughter. Many
years have passed since then, and my daughter has forgiven me,
but I still regret it. At least I can thank God that I learned something
from it.

LET'S TALK: What about you? What is lacking in your life? Are
there people you have grown impatient with? Do you have them in
mind? Begin to make yourself aware of the love of God for them. Let
the Patient One do His work in us, and watch what happens.

Good Deeds

In the same way, let your good deeds shine out for all to see, so that everyone will praise your heavenly Father. → Matthew 5:16

When I was on a mini trip to Florida with my girlfriends, the friend who was hosting us knew how much I love lighthouses, so we took her golf cart to see one on the shore nearby. It was incredible to see it up close, and my delight seemed to grow the closer we got. The building was important as a historical landmark, but its practical function was even greater: At one time, sailors out at sea had relied on this beacon to shine, to guide them home, and to keep them from running the ship aground.

It was a living metaphor for Jesus's adamancy in making sure we know our great purpose. Not only is He the Light that guides us home and keeps us from wrecking our ships, He also tasks us to beam His light to the world through our good deeds for a magnificent purpose—so that everyone will be directed to our Heavenly Father.

LET'S TALK: How have you noticed the Holy Spirit guiding you to shine by doing good? As you go to the Lord, ask Him in what ways you can shine for His glory today.

Writing Prompts

Are you tired? Worn out? Burned out on religion? Come to me . . . Walk with me and work with me—watch how I do it. Learn the unforced rhythms of grace. I won't lay anything heavy or ill-fitting on you. Keep company with me and you'll learn to live freely and lightly. → Matthew 11:28–30 (MSG)

Do you ever feel burned out? I know I do sometimes. In fact, I was struggling just to finish writing this devotional! I texted a dear friend and said, "If you're led, could you send me writing prompts? Whatever word you get, will you text me?"

After sending that text, I sat there staring at the computer—until I was interrupted by the Holy Spirit reminding me of all the times God had helped me with this problem before. I thought of the moments when God was teaching me to draw and paint, and how everything was done in worship. None of it felt like work; it just flowed. In that moment, the Holy Spirit reminded me that I just needed to worship Him, and my creativity would begin to flow again.

In that moment, I asked the Lord, "What song would you like me to worship with?" The only thing I "heard" was the word "breathe." The only issue was that I couldn't recall a song by that title. But when I opened up the music app on my phone, there it was: "Breathe." And now, as I type these words, God is ministering to me, and I get to minister to Him in worship, allowing Him to be my breath, my wind of refreshment, and my favorite writing prompt.

TRY THIS TODAY: Have you been doing things with a "grind" mentality? Are you getting exhausted? It's likely that the worship element has been taken out of the equation. Today, be reminded by God's Word to do everything as unto the Lord, ministering to the heart of God. By default, everything else will be taken care of. Try it, and just watch what happens!

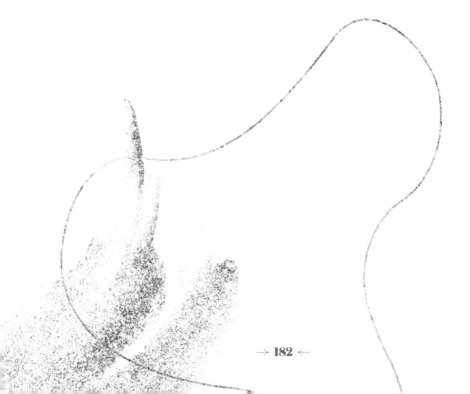

Faith That Binds

Then Jesus said to the disciples,
"Have faith in God." → Mark 11:22

Have you ever noticed that when you're worshiping the Lord with fervent praise, all the worries and fears in the forefront of your mind just bow before the King of Glory? Even if you've been dragging your feet and procrastinating on worship, once you get started, the narrative shifts, the voices become silent, and you suddenly see your fears for what they really were: illusions, a mirage with no substance. Faith stirs and causes every mountain to be moved, every foe to bow, and every weapon to have no power.

That doesn't mean you're ignoring your fears or pretending they're not there. It's just that you recognize distractions for what they really are and refuse to give them power as you breathe and speak the power of God over your life and others'. The atmosphere in that moment changes, and you find yourself standing in the authority of Christ as an heir of God, in a place of God's righteousness in Christ Jesus. And all of it starts with obedience to worship God, even if everything in you didn't want to.

LET'S PRAY: "Father God, thank You for binding us to You in faith—faith in who You are, faith to tell the mountains to move, and faith that every crooked thing will be made straight by You. In Jesus's name, amen."

The Door

I am the door. → John 10:9 (NKJV)

One day, I was chatting on the phone with a friend while I did laundry. I moved the clothes from the washer to the dryer on autopilot, barely looking as I tossed in a dryer sheet and pressed the power button. Seconds later, I heard a loud banging sound coming from inside the dryer. "What the heck?" I said to my friend. I opened the dryer door . . . and let out a scream as my cat jumped out!

Yes, my cat had apparently gotten into the dryer when I wasn't looking and spent a few seconds taking the ride of his life. He was ultimately just fine, but we were both a bit shaken up.

How many times have we, like that cat, jumped into spaces that we were never meant to jump into? How many times have we done things we know we shouldn't—like complain about problems in life instead of changing our perspectives and seeing what we do have, rather than what we don't? And how many times have we justified it by telling ourselves, "Well, the door wouldn't be open if I weren't supposed to walk through it."

Sometimes, doors aren't meant to be walked through, even when they're wide open. Intimacy with God, on the other hand, has the power to make us realize that He is the door. When we remain in Him and quiet ourselves before Him, He will make known where we're supposed to go, because He is the Way.

> **TRY THIS TODAY:** Are there doors open before you right now? Have you reached out to the One who is the true door? The One who is the Way? Go to Him in this moment, no matter what you're doing, and just acknowledge Him as the Way. Then go about your activities, fully aware of His presence.

Creation's Resounding Echo of Awe

I can never escape from your Spirit!
I can never get away from your presence!
→ Psalm 139:7

For some reason, on this particular day, the sky really caught my attention. The brilliant blue expanse was incredibly vast. I couldn't stop staring at the beautiful patterns of the cloud coverage. Everything was bright and clear, and the rays of the sun seemed to join the symphony of praise within the skies. It almost felt like a private moment with creation.

Today's scripture reminds me of the magnificent truth that I can never escape from God's Spirit. Creation itself is a resounding reminder that we can never get away from God's presence, from hearing the birds effortlessly sing to seeing the endless sky above. How often have we ignored the glory of such things before us every day? Seriously, think about it. The beauty of this sky is above us every day, being held in place by God—yet we can't trust Him with our own issues? I want to look at the sky this way every day, so that I never get away from the awareness of God's presence.

LET'S TALK: Do you need that reminder today that no matter what you do, you just can't get away from God? He's right there with you. No matter what you're doing, wherever you're reading this, He's surrounding you. Now is the time to take notice of His presence. Do you sense His nearness?

Are You Willing?

But to you who are willing to listen, I say, love your enemies! Do good to those who hate you.
→ Luke 6:27

Recently, my daughter and I were in one of our favorite restaurants enjoying our mother-daughter time. As we sat at our table eating our chips and salsa, we heard a woman blurting out expletives at her husband. The man's demeanor noticeably sank as he sat there in his booth. My heart sank, too, and I could see in my daughter's eyes that she was angry. I thought I might have to hold her back from getting up and telling this woman off!

I prayed God would use me to show this woman what was what. But today's scripture came up in my spirit, and it was as though I was being physically held down. I started to make excuses for why I didn't have to love her as I was commanded to do: "She's not *my* enemy, she's *his*, so this doesn't apply to me." But then I heard the Lord saying in my heart, "Overcome evil by doing good. Pay for their dinner." My first thought was "No way!" But I had prayed to be utilized by God, and here was an opportunity for Him to be seen. It wasn't what I had in mind when I prayed that prayer, but I couldn't argue with it.

I quietly asked the server to let me pay for their check without letting them know it was us. When the woman found out the check had been paid, she was livid. She got up from the table, cursed her husband, and stormed out. I thought, *Lord, I don't think that was a good idea.* But then I heard these words: "To love your enemies is to pray, 'Father forgive them for they know not what they do.'"

It didn't turn out the way I expected, but when God shares with us to do something, we do it simply to obey, not for the results. Even though I didn't get to see the effects of my obedience, it doesn't mean that God wasn't working. Maybe God used that moment to reach the server, the onlookers, the couple when they thought back on it later, or even my daughter and me. No matter what, I got to sow a seed of blessing, and the return on that is beyond imagination.

LET'S PRAY: "Father, thank You that I am Your daughter, a vessel, set apart and useful for the Master, prepared for every good work. In Jesus's name, amen."

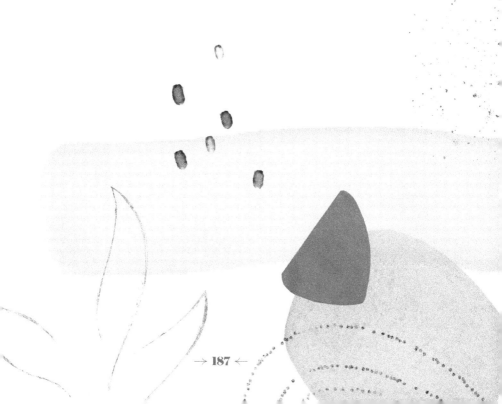

Squeezed

Your love for one another will prove to the world that you are my disciples. → John 13:35

When I squeezed a lemon, it came as no surprise that I got lemon juice. When I squeezed an orange, it came as no surprise that orange juice came splashing out. When I placed garlic in the garlic press, surprisingly, a banana emerged. Just kidding, of course. That wouldn't happen. It would be crazy, right?

So I've been asking myself why it is that when I'm squeezed by those who have offended me, what comes out isn't evidence of whom I say I belong to. What comes out is my reaction, not the promises of God. When I get squeezed, why is Jesus not being seen through me? Sometimes, it's hard to yield to the Holy Spirit, who produces the fruit of love. When we're squeezed by the trials of this life, we must learn to actively respond to God, rather than to the issue at hand. When we go to the Lord and set our hearts before Him, we can see the matter at hand with God's loving perspective. Then we get to reveal Him instead of ourselves.

LET'S PRAY: "Father, thank You that I was a sinner saved by grace and now You call me a saint. Thank You that when the squeezings of life come, I get to be Your child and demonstrate Your love. In Jesus's name, amen."

A Joyful Spectacle

Be careful to live properly among
your unbelieving neighbors. Then even
if they accuse you of doing wrong, they will
see your honorable behavior, and they
will give honor to God when he judges
the world. → 1 Peter 2:12

Wronged. Hurt. Used.

You'd better do something about it.

Fight! Fight! Fight!

Get distracted!

A life of constant warring. No peace. Fighting with idle words that produce no life. In the eyes of so many people, this way is the only way.

Yet in a moment, suddenly, God's supernatural insight reveals an "out-of-this-world" peace like no other. It's the kind of revelation that makes a joyful spectacle, leaving people in awe, as though they just saw a grandiose fireworks display. Suddenly you realize: All that fighting was for nothing. *This* is what the Kingdom of God looks like when it invades the earth. It lights up the world!

When Jesus said that we are the light of the world, He didn't say it so that we would talk about how dark the world is. He meant to show the people of the world how bright we are. He wanted us to see how that brightness helps us glorify our Father God, as our good deeds on earth tell others whom we belong to. When we realize how good God is, we just can't help but reflect His light by doing good to others. Overcome evil with good. This is what the Kingdom of God is all about.

LET'S PRAY: "Father God, You have identified Your children as the light of the world, so allow me to be aware of the revelation that You live within me. I want to be so blown away that You live within me that my life will cause others to want You. Lord, no matter what is done to me, let my responses be from You and You alone! In Jesus's name, amen."

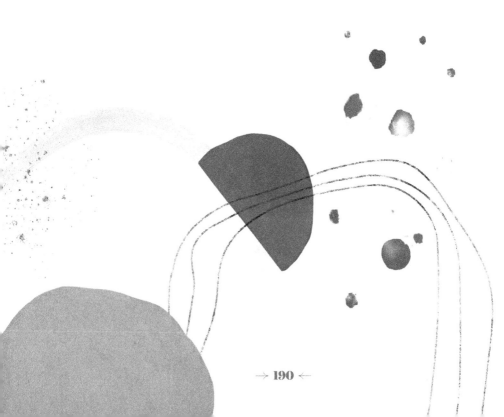

The Finish Line

I press on to reach the end of the race
and receive the heavenly prize for which
God, through Christ Jesus, is calling us.
→ Philippians 3:14

Recently, I was running along a trail—actually more like speed walking. Okay, so I was really just walking. But still, I noticed my mind's natural desire to press onward toward the finish line. It was a clear goal, and I couldn't help but want to reach it.

At first, it reminded me of pressing into the Lord. But then I realized that life with God is more like running around a track—it's a full circle. As we run forward from Him as our starting point, we're also running back toward Him. The starting line is the finish line, just as God is the First and the Last. And no matter how many times we run that loop, we can't help but want to do it again.

Then I began thinking about what repentance looks like. When the Holy Spirit convicts us of something we have done wrong, we don't feel shame. Instead, as my friend Mac says, it's simply an invitation to come to the Father. There is no groveling involved, just a knowledge that He forgives us. As we receive His forgiveness, we put the old way of doing things down and actively turn away, choosing instead to turn to the Father God so that we can receive the grace to obey Him. We run toward Him as our finishing line so He can simultaneously be a new start for us. It's an active forward motion not just with Him but in Him, because He is not only the beginning and the end—He is also the journey.

TRY THIS TODAY: Have you been scared to repent? Are you too embarrassed to admit that something you've done was not God's way after all? I promise it's not as scary as it might seem. It's actually freeing! Just go to Him now and let Him know you're sorry for whatever it is you want to receive forgiveness for. He's waiting. And once you do it, you'll feel the burdens removed. I'm cheering for you. It's so worth it.

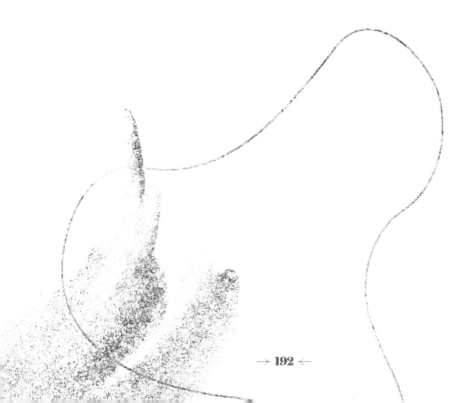

The Storyline

Righteousness and justice are the foundation of your throne. Unfailing love and truth walk before you as attendants. → Psalm 89:14

I had just finished reading a book to the kids during story time at the local library when one little boy's hand shot up. He asked a question, and I answered it. Then another child's hand went up, then another. Soon we weren't even talking about the book anymore. We were completely off-topic, going on about popcorn and root beer. I giggle as I think about their little discussions. Their imaginations were soaring, and they were really enjoying story time. But as the children's volume increased, I finally said, "Wow! We have a lot of great stories, but for now, let's all put our hands down and use our library voices. Shhh." It was time to reset and get back to the storyline.

I can be like those little children sometimes, excited to learn about the Lord. As I allow the Lord to teach me, my questions begin, and I go from asking about who He is to getting off-topic and asking something else. I might be reading the Bible and then suddenly, instead of focusing on God's Word, I'm thinking, *Why did David, of all people, fall for Bathsheba?* Of course, those kinds of questions aren't wrong. We can learn from them. But, like the sweet children in the library, eventually I need to focus, spending less time thinking about the character flaws of an individual in the Bible and more time on how that person's story reveals the steadfast character of God. It's evidence that God is unchanging, everlasting, and immovable in character. He comes through in the moments of questioning, even when I don't see it.

LET'S PRAY: "Father, thank You for Your steadfastness. You are majestic, holy, and unchanging through the changing of the ages. Please help me return to that fact again and again, no matter how my mind wanders. In Jesus's name, amen."

Lessons from Dirt

Other seeds fell on shallow soil with underlying rock. The seeds sprouted quickly because the soil was shallow. But the plants soon wilted under the hot sun, and since they didn't have deep roots, they died. → Matthew 13:5–6

I wanted to grow some flowers in my yard, but digging through the ground to plant the seeds seemed next to impossible. There was limestone less than an inch below the surface; the ground was just too hard. Eventually, I changed tactics, buying terra cotta pots and potting soil so that the seeds could bloom into flowers there instead.

The parable of the farmer scattering seed in Matthew 13 came to mind. In that parable, Jesus tells us how different seeds did or didn't grow, based on various conditions of their environment—rocky soil, the presence of birds, and so on. The seeds represent the Word of God and how it is received, successfully or unsuccessfully, in different people's hearts. When I had initially attempted to plant those seeds, I was getting a lesson about the condition of my own heart. Was my heart soft and pliable, receiving truth from God's Word like potting soil? Or was it as hard as limestone?

I set it in my heart to want to be soil that is soft and fertile, nurturing God's life-giving Word in my soul. In those moments, the Holy Spirit revealed that the way to ensure my heart is continually rich is to be in awe of Him at every moment. That de-magnifies the issues of life and magnifies God's glorious greatness, allowing me to receive His Word at every given moment and to be transformed to be more like Him on a continual basis.

LET'S PRAY: "Father God, thank You for being the farmer of my heart. Ensure that the condition of my heart is fertile and pliable to receive Your truth that changes me to look more like You. I want to be a sign of Your wonder-working power. In Jesus's name, amen."

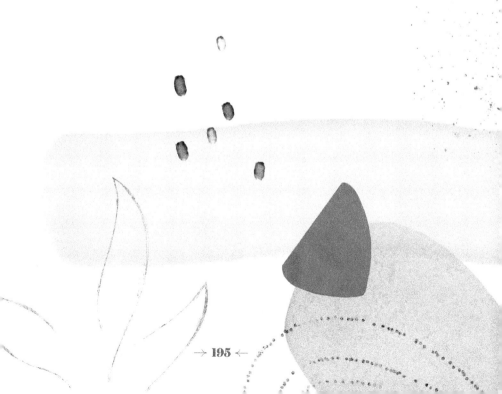

Going Live

For the word of God is alive and powerful.
It is sharper than the sharpest two-edged
sword, cutting between soul and spirit,
between joint and marrow. It exposes our
innermost thoughts and desires.
→ Hebrews 4:12

I was "going live"—broadcasting a live video on social media—to share an analogy on my ministry page. But as I clicked on the app, what I wanted to share switched from my own ideas to God's. To be completely transparent, if I'd had any idea what was about to take place, I quite possibly wouldn't have hit the LIVE VIDEO button.

Here's what happened next: I repented for falling for and helping spread a narrative that pushed a human agenda instead of a godly one. I apologized for unintentionally leading people away from God by trying to deal with injustice, when God wants to do that by spreading His love. As I finished up the video and replayed it, my eyes just about popped out of my head, but telling the truth was so freeing, and some of my viewers even commented that they were also convicted.

Today's scripture is so true. God's truth is as a very sharp, two-edged sword. It precisely divides earthly agendas from divine ones, yet it brings peace at the same time.

LET'S PRAY: "Father God, thank You for Your life-giving Word that severs lies to reveal the truth. There's no question when I see the truth revealed with Your Word by Your Spirit. In Jesus's name, amen."

Not Learning at Someone Else's Expense

Don't be selfish; don't try to impress others.
Be humble, thinking of others as better
than yourselves. → Philippians 2:3

Early on, in my younger years of being in ministry, I was zealous, but I didn't always express that with the Holy Spirit's love, and I would often be unintentionally inconsiderate of others. Once, our women's group had been praying over a beautiful woman who had not been able to get pregnant. One day, she pulled me aside and privately told me that she was so grateful for our prayers and that she was finally pregnant. I was thrilled—and in my immaturity, proud of being the first to know, I took it upon myself to start sharing her news.

A few weeks later, as we were setting up for a women's conference, an older woman approached me and pointed her finger at me. With tears in her eyes, she said, "Why would you tell everyone that my daughter was pregnant? Do you know how many people have called to congratulate her? She's not pregnant!"

I felt the blood leave my face. I must have misheard what this woman's daughter had told me. I wanted to kick myself. "I'm so sorry," I said. "Please forgive me. Where is your daughter, is she here?" Still upset, she led me to where her daughter was. I looked her straight in the eyes and deeply apologized. This precious woman said, "When I saw you that day, I did not tell you I was pregnant. And even if I did, what would make you think it was okay to tell anyone?"

That moment has been seared in my memory, not out of condemnation but out of a prayer—my prayer to God to not be so selfish and prideful that I try to impress others by knowing information they don't. I learned my lesson, but at the expense of hurting someone else. Next time, I hope to simply learn from the Lord and His Word.

LET'S TALK: Perhaps you would never have done what I did, but we've all made our mistakes. And though we all learn the hard way at times, scripture like today's is a great reminder of many lessons. How has today's scripture made you want to respond to the Lord? How has today's devotion caused you to see a particular situation in your life differently?

Cleaning Out the Closet

Create in me a clean heart, O God.
Renew a loyal spirit within me. → Psalm 51:10

If you're anything like me, cleaning out your closet is no easy task. The last time I did it, I had no idea how much stuff was crammed in there, hidden from my eyes, until I had emptied the entire closet. I stared in disbelief at the piles and piles of bags, photos, artwork, tissue paper from Christmas . . . all sorts of junk that I hadn't used in a long time and knew I would never use again.

As I got rid of all that stuff, it felt like such a revelatory analogy about the things hidden in my heart—all those buried issues I usually have no idea that I have. I imagined myself allowing God into my heart to clear out all my baggage, revealing His heart in its place. His heart is so holy and pure, it causes me to see that the brokenness I've held on to wasn't a gift from Him at all. It was just junk. May the beauty of His love for us be enough to say, "I surrender it all to You, Lord."

LET'S PRAY: "Yes, Lord, I surrender all to You. You are so worthy to be praised! That You would allow me to know Your heart is so loving. Thank You for getting the junk out. In Jesus's name, amen."

Willing Conversations

> If another believer sins against you, go privately and point out the offense. If the other person listens and confesses it, you have won that person back. → Matthew 18:15

My phone lit up with a message notification. It was from a friend I hadn't seen or talked to in a long time. She wanted to have a conversation with me about some things I'd posted on social media. At first, I was really scared. Condemning thoughts swarmed me. What had I said?

We scheduled a phone conversation. I asked whether it would be the kind of call where I needed to just listen or one in which she invited a dialogue. She immediately texted, "I want a dialogue. I want to hear what you have to say."

At that, the Holy Spirit turned my fear into awe. I was amazed at my friend's willingness to have a conversation with me, rather than just cutting me off or "unfriending" me. Our conversation ended up being incredibly life-giving. The Holy Spirit ministered to both of us as we spoke for almost two hours. It was refreshing to realize that we were both open to hear His heart and that the love of God was powerfully evident. We were able to communicate openly and honestly, and I was even able to be transparent and share how God revealed my heart even after I'd already posted the things my friend was struck by. It was such a powerful moment, and one that I will remember as the beautiful picture of a friend in Christ.

LET'S TALK: Is there someone in your life you're fearful to have a conversation with? Perhaps you're afraid because the relationship could end, but have you considered that you might also win the person back? Isn't it worth trying? As you give the situation to the Lord, be aware of doing this to honor Him. And no matter how it turns out, just know You were given the grace to obey.

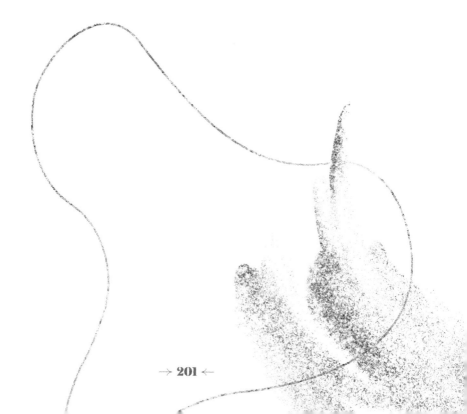

Content with Whatever

I have learned how to be content with whatever I have. I know how to live on almost nothing or with everything. I have learned the secret of living in every situation, whether it is with a full stomach or empty, with plenty or little. → Philippians 4:11–12

I love today's scripture, in which Paul shows the boldness of believing in God. His adamant grace to be content in any manner of living shows that God is his portion in every aspect of life, whether he has little or much.

Can you imagine having that mindset while in prison? Paul was imprisoned many times, sometimes in very harsh conditions. He learned to be content even when he was surrounded by filth and sewage, even when he had disease-infested critters as his cell mates. (Just the thought of it gives me the heebie-jeebies!) His attitude did not bend to his circumstances; instead, his circumstances bowed to the truth of God. This is evidence of a life lived with eyes fixed on the Lord. This is what I want. Let us keep our perspective trained on the Lord.

LET'S PRAY: "Lord, give me the perspective to see You in suffering so completely that I don't even see the suffering because I'm fixed on You. Let me see myself not as a resident of this world but as a citizen of heaven. In Jesus's name, amen."

Antidote to Worry

Are any of you suffering hardships?
You should pray. Are any of you happy?
You should sing praises. → James 5:13

There was a time when fear was my residence, worry was my landlord, and chaos and mayhem were my regular visitors. It was self-destructive to inhabit this unhealthy headspace, but a soft inner voice told me lies: that everyone lived this way, that it was just the way things were. I believed it, until the day I read today's scripture. I couldn't believe there was a simple but profound antidote to fear: prayer.

Have you ever thought, "You mean I have to pray about this *again*? Haven't I already prayed about it enough?" If so, let me send you a reminder like the one I received. Praying is not something we *have to* do, it's something we *get to* do. We're not just talking to God—we're allowing Him to talk to us. These moments of thankfulness heighten our awareness of who God is. Bravery rises up inside of us, and we're able to experience God's peace. We no longer hear the voice of worry, because we're opened up completely to God's voice of truth.

LET'S PRAY: "Father, thank You for the ability to pray and dialogue with You and Your Word. Your antidote to worry is simply to pray. I give my awareness to You, Lord, and ask You to heighten it so I can be divinely distracted by You. In Jesus's name, amen."

You Have a Voice

A time to tear and a time to mend. A time to be quiet and a time to speak. → Ecclesiastes 3:7

Our daughter, Tristin, has an innate ability to speak her mind. When she was about 17 years old, we overheard her holding her own with her older brother. He loves and respects her, but he also knows exactly how to push her buttons. He never does it out of malice—he does it because he loves her sass. But now, suddenly, she started to raise her voice and speak in a manner that wasn't kind or loving.

At just the right time, her dad interrupted with his steady, deep voice. "Tristin! I need you to come over here right now. Take a seat." She hesitantly joined him at the table. Tristin respects her father so much that he doesn't have to do anything but call her name and she listens.

He leaned in close and said, "Tristin, I want you to know that I hear you and I value your voice. I don't want anyone to ever convince you that your voice is not valued, because it is so valuable. However, you need to know that there is a time and a place for it, and the way you were using it just now was not appropriate. Do you understand?"

With tears streaming, she said, "Yes, Dad." He got up and gave her a hug.

The way her dad let her know that he valued her voice and guided her in knowing how and when to use it was a beautiful picture of today's scripture. It reminded me of God's desire to hear and guide us.

LET'S PRAY: "Father God, thank You for the strengths that are innately within me in Jesus's name. Holy Spirit, I am so grateful to You for showing me the weak spots and how You want to use them for Your glory to point others forward and upward to You. In Jesus's name, amen."

Approved

Obviously, I'm not trying to win the approval of people, but of God. If pleasing people were my goal, I would not be Christ's servant.
→ Galatians 1:10

When I was in my 20s and 30s, my life goal was for everyone to like me—even if I didn't like them. I constantly sought and pleaded for approval, to the point of exhaustion. It was an ego-driven lifestyle, and as I got older and wiser, I began to realize it was getting me nowhere fast. Then I had a moment of awakening—I received the revelation that I was God's daughter, which meant I was already accepted and approved of, before I could even earn it.

From this moment of waking up, an overwhelming awe marked my heart as it opened to the heart of the Father. His approval marks me as His. This beautiful knowing quashed the desire to win the approval of others. Earthly approval is immaterial because, as today's scripture says, if pleasing people were my goal, it would be proof that I didn't belong to Him. And I don't want anything else but to know I am His and He is mine.

LET'S PRAY: "Father, thank You for Your approval from before I was even born. Lord, let this knowing set a fire in every part of my heart. A heart for You, my affections exalting You as the desire for approval is replaced with the desire for You. In Jesus's name, amen."

Humble Yourself

Pride ends in humiliation,
while humility brings honor.
→ Proverbs 29:23

Recently, while going over some things I've been actively learning from the Lord, I wrote this down: "We must never intentionally or unintentionally exploit others who have been wronged in an attempt to settle our own unsettled hurts. When others have been hurt, we can't pretend to be standing with them if we're really just trying to relieve the bitterness within our own resistant hearts."

Have you ever done this? Do you perhaps parent your children from this place sometimes? When your kids are hurt by others, do you use it as an opportunity to get back at those who hurt you?

When I looked at the words I'd written, I was surprised to realize that this was something I had done many times over the years but had never before put into words. I had valued my prideful stance more than I valued humbling myself before the mighty power of God. I had not wanted to surrender those hidden places that were being exposed.

If you can surrender the pain to God instead, you will begin raising up children of God who are unoffendable. You will teach them how to pray for those who hurt them and watch God do what only He can do.

When God led me to write those words, it was beautiful to see how He had worked on my heart and urged me to reveal His love to anyone He sends me to. Let me remind you as I was reminded: When we humble ourselves, we give all our worries to Him, as it reveals we truly know He cares.

TRY THIS TODAY: Are there some unresolved hurts within your heart you haven't yet surrendered? Literally surrender them, by lifting your hands up as though raising up the pain to God. Say, "It's Yours now, Lord; I trade it in for Your love and forgiveness."

Jesus Is True Perspective

Don't copy the behavior and customs of this world, but let God transform you into a new person by changing the way you think.
→ Romans 12:2

It's one thing to look at life from our own perspective, but it's another to see things from someone else's point of view. And it's something else entirely to see from our perspective in Jesus Christ. The key is to look *to* and *at* Jesus. When everyone else begins waving their arms and shouting, "Look over here," let that be an indicator that it's time to look even more to Jesus.

How do we look to Jesus? We open up the Bible and let Him truly speak to us as we read, because reading the Word of God is listening to Him. There might be moments when people are upset that you're not paying attention to what they want you to pay attention to. Don't be offended or annoyed; just let that be a reminder to keep your focus on Christ and simply be a doer of God's love. See, speak, and hear from a place of intimacy with Jesus, instead of copying the behavior and customs of this world. If you do this, you will be letting God transform the way you think.

LET'S PRAY: "Father God, thank You for being my help whenever I look to You. You transform me into a new person as You change the way I think. In Jesus's name, amen."

Acknowledgments

I must express my gratefulness to You, Lord. All those years ago on March 6, 2003, I awakened to You, and my life has been transformed in ways I never thought possible. Thank You for the countless moments in which I have learned who You are as the author and finisher of my faith. Let the pages of this book reveal my awe of You.

To my husband, Tim, you have loved me and supported me so uniquely. Your presence alone has caused me to stay fixed on Jesus as you encouraged me to write and reminded me often of the God I do this with and for.

To my beautiful daughter, Tristin, I am so grateful to God that I unknowingly raised up one of my best friends. What a blessing to do this life with you, speaking truth to one another and being bold and brave in our faith in God with one another.

Sweet thankfulness to my son, Cody. I'm so excited to see the continual unfolding of what you allow God to do in your beautiful family's life. What a blessing to know you, Jennifer, and our sweet grandbaby, Nicholas. I still remember when you were about 15 years old and you invested $20 in me to finish my first book. That will be a memory I hold all of my days.

I am also so grateful to God for the family I was raised in. Dad, we entered our first writing contest together on Mother's Day in 1980, when I was five years old, and our submission won first place. Of course, it was truly your work, but you let me believe it was my own. You also bought my first typewriter in 1987, knowing that I would write one day, even though my abilities didn't yet line up with your belief. Mom, you are a prayer warrior who is bold and tenacious in your faith to know His redeeming power. The way you believe in God would make giants bow. Your life reveals the beautiful handprints of God. What a

blessing. And to my beautiful sisters who have prayed for me often and encouraged me to write, there are no other sisters I would rather have than the two of you.

I also must write my gratitude to my "mother-in-love," Kennetha, and my "brothers-in-love," Greg and Jeff, as well as their beautiful families! Thank you for loving me and encouraging me to be who I am in the Lord.

I am thankful for my countless friends who have prayed for me during the writing of this book. You know who you are, and I'm blessed by Jesus to have you in my life.

I'm so grateful for my Instagram and Facebook supporters who helped me get this devotional out there. Thank you to everyone who has shared it with friends and family or via social media. Even what you might deem small gestures are life-changing and incredibly significant for me.

Last but not least, I'd like to thank the amazing team at Rockridge Press for staying true to my writing voice. The way you placed my words together so eloquently will only cause people to want our God more.

About the Author

TERESA ANN CRISWELL is a joy-filled woman who loves being a wife to her husband of 22 years as well as a mom, grandma, and "mother-in-love." She is the founder and host of the podcast, YouTube channel, and blog *Let's Talk with Teresa Ann* and the *OH . . . Teresa and Tristin Podcast*, which she produces with her daughter. Her previous books include *God Is Enthralled by Your Beauty* and *Heavenly Wit*.